Advances in Contemporary Educational Thought Series
Jonas F. Soltis, Editor

DYING
TO
TEACH

*The Educator's Search
for Immortality*

DAVID J. BLACKER

Teachers College, Columbia University
New York and London

Published by Teachers College Press, 1234 Amsterdam Avenue, New York, NY 10027

Portions of Chapter 1 first appeared in substantially different form in ''Education as the Normative Dimension of Philosophical Hermeneutics,'' *Proceedings of the Philosophy of Education Society*, 1993.

Portions of Chapter 1 also appear in substantially different form in ''Education as Immortality: Toward the Rehabilitation of an Ideal,'' *Religious Education*, forthcoming.

Portions of Chapter 4 first appeared in substantially different form in ''Education as Immortality: Classical and Contemporary Pathways,'' *Proceedings of the Philosophy of Education Society*, 1995.

Quotation from ''Van Gogh Gives Evidence,'' by Evá Tóth, which appeared in English translation in *American Poetry Review* (1995), is used with permission of the author.

Quotations from Martha Nussbaum, *The Therapy of Desire: Theory and Practice in Hellenistic Ethics*, Copyright © 1994 by Princeton University Press. Reprinted by permission of Princeton University Press.

Library of Congress Cataloging-in-Publication Data

Blacker, David J.
    Dying to teach : the educator's search for immortality / David J. Blacker
        p.   cm. — (Advances in contemporary educational thought series ; v. 18)
    Includes bibliographical references and index.
    ISBN 0-8077-3592-2 (alk. paper)
        1. Teaching—Philosophy. 2. Education—Philosophy. 3. Teachers.
    4. Immortality. I. Title. II. Series.
    LB1025.3.B58 1997
    371.102'01—dc21   96-40843

ISBN 0-8077-3592-2 (cloth)

Printed on acid-free paper
Manufactured in the United States of America

04 03 02 01 00 99 98 97   8 7 6 5 4 3 2 1

Are you holding
the universe? You hold
onto my smallness. How do you grasp it,
how does it not
slip away?

—Denise Levertov

Contents

Foreword

Teaching is a universal human activity carried out by human beings in every culture, time, and place. It takes many forms and has been characterized by many metaphors, some complimentary and some derogatory. Juxtaposed to teacher as artist, as mentor, as guide, as nurturer are teacher as banker, as filler of empty vessels, as disciplinarian. In Western literature, for every Socrates-like teacher engaging students in thought-provoking dialogue, there is a Dickensian Mr. Gradgrind demanding meaningless definitional recitations. How teachers "see" teaching determines to a large extent how they *act* as teachers.

In this book, David Blacker explores a highly unusual image of teaching as immortality in a new way. Living on in one's students by having given them something of oneself is not an uncommon idea. Nor is the idea of helping students and oneself approach the eternal by engaging in the pursuit of Truth. But Blacker treats these ideas as dialectical and seeks a Hegelian synthesis of them by developing the image of immortality as an atemporal, mythic, meaning-making, relational enterprise. Teaching as immortality is a difficult and complex concept to grasp, but Blacker takes the reader through Greek and Roman philosophers, Judeo-Christian beliefs about immortality, Heideggerian existentialism, and Gadamer's hermeneutics with a graceful, engaging, and illuminating writing style that makes sense of this rich image.

This is a book for anyone who wants to enlarge their view of teaching and who appreciates the contribution that a nontechnical treatment of relevant philosophy can make to our understanding of perennial aspects of everyday life.

Jonas F. Soltis
Series Editor

Acknowledgments

True to the spirit of this book, there are many who made it possible. Overall, my theoretical orientation is powerfully shaped by Martin Heidegger and Hans-Georg Gadamer. It is difficult to admit the former, honestly, given my repugnance toward what I regard as his political and moral crimes. But what am I to do? I cannot escape his grip, ambivalent as my allegiance may be. The latter is, to me, the truest embodiment of a latter-day Socrates; I find so much there that is simultaneously challenging, yet hopeful and humane.

Closer to hand, the project was given courage and color by an eclectically interdisciplinary crew: the philosopher Martha Nussbaum, the social theorist Zygmunt Bauman, the novelist Milan Kundera, the historian of religion Mircea Eliade, the psychologist Carol Gilligan, and the poet Theodore Roethke. Each of these thinkers at key points led me to see things I would not have seen alone.

A number of individuals have been generous with their time and their intellect in critiquing drafts of part or all of the manuscript: Nicholas Burbules, Walter Feinberg, Gary Fenstermacher, C. H. George, Jessica George, Margaret George, Thomas Green, Allen Hance, Kevin McDonough, Judith Mogilka, David O'Connor, Ralph Page, Jonas Soltis, and Peter Winch. Each of these persons has improved the manuscript, though, of course, its many remaining faults are all too inescapably mine and mine alone. I am honored to have read parts of the manuscript before the Philosophy of Education Society, the American Educational Studies Association, the University of Illinois Philosophy of Education Discussion Group, the Ball State University Foundations of Education Discussion Group, the Illinois State University Administrator's Club, and to more captive "audiences" in several undergraduate and graduate courses at Illinois State. I am grateful to all on those occasions who thought my work worth listening to and to the many who made those lively discussions go.

At Teachers College Press, Micah Kleit, Jonas Soltis, and Faye Zucker have earned my lasting gratitude and appreciation. I thank them all for taking a chance on an admittedly off-the-beaten-path manuscript, shepherding it through the acceptance and production process, and Faye for, in addition, providing psychological aid and comfort to a nervous, perhaps even at times neurotic, first-time author. Peter Sieger, Lori Tate, and Karen Osborne were prompt, pleasant, and professional in helping me prepare the final manuscript. A wonderful and talented group they all are.

A debt of an altogether different kind goes to my family: my sisters, Nancy and Mimi, my beloved wife and daughter, Jessica and Abigail, and, as I write, the newly emergent life that is my son, Joshua. The word *debt* scarcely captures what I owe to them all, as is true of what is joyfully owed my mother and father, Marcia Blacker and H. Martin Blacker, to whom this book is dedicated.

DYING
TO
TEACH

*The Educator's Search
for Immortality*

CHAPTER 1

Education and the Longing for Immortality

A teacher affects eternity; he can never tell where his influence stops.

—*Henry Adams (1907/1990)*

EDUCATION AS IMMORTALITY

My father, a teacher of medicine and mentor to countless students, residents, and colleagues, once told me that his immortality would consist in his influence on those he had taught. Hearing this surprised me as a 16-year-old, especially in light of the observant Jewish upbringing he had helped see to for my sisters and me. I was even more surprised when he told me that he had inherited this idea from my grandfather, someone I had always thought of as more observant still. And who knows where *he* got it? Did the conspiracy go back to Abraham, I wondered? So father, grandfather, and however many additional ancestors unnamed did not harbor the orthodox religious beliefs I had always ascribed to them by default. And what's more, they both located whatever was enduring about themselves in something so this-worldly as to seem rather anticlimactic, rather disappointing to me, at the time an agnostic yet still-hopeful adolescent. I must have responded with something like, "You mean that's *it*? Your influence on others? Your *teaching*?"

The banality of my patriarchs! What could be behind such ideas?

As it turns out, I've come to believe a great deal lies behind them indeed, and hardly any of it now seems banal. I would like to make the case, in fact, that my father's sentiment has in the Western tradition a long and even ancient history to it, extending at least to Socrates, philosophy's archetypal nonmentoring mentor. It is, as I shall argue, one strand in a braid that coils in and out of the history of education and philosophy—sometimes hidden, sometimes not. This is the idea, captured in my father's feeling of living on through his teaching, that via the enterprise of education writ large one can secure a kind of immortality beyond one's physical–temporal existence. Here lies a motivation, the psychologist might say, at times powerful yet mostly unacknowledged. Milan Kundera (1992), the Czech novelist, writes that there "is a certain part of us that lives outside of time. Perhaps we become aware of our age only at exceptional moments and most of the time we are ageless" (p. 4). My aim here is to say something concerning a long yet mostly ignored tradition in educational thought echoing this sentiment, one that forges a link between teaching and learning on the one hand and that which is "ageless" and "outside of time" on the other.

In teaching and learning, I believe, we are immortal. Yet for most of us—and for all of us most of the time—our awareness of this is impaired. As, of course, it always does, immortality eludes us. But still it waits. It always waits for us. My book means to show something of how this is so.

CLASSICAL ROOTS

This vision of education as immortality has, however, been subject to two quite different—from time to time even competing—formulations. These two formulations make an early appearance unified in the person of Socrates, although they are straight away split apart by Plato, who seizes in his own post-Socratic writings upon but half of the "original" Socratic vision. The other half, the one Plato mostly discards, reflects sensibilities consistent with the notorious Sophists, the itinerant pay-per-view teachers of rhetoric and worldly success whom Plato famously vilifies. Since being split apart, both halves of the parent Socratic vision have been widely and enduringly influential on their own, and occasionally in tandem. Taken together, they comprise two aspects of one of the most powerful motivating factors for why one would want to engage in teaching at all. It is a motivation little discussed, however, as if it might sound embarrassingly occult or perhaps selfish: the longing for immortality.

What are these two halves, then?

The first is the Platonic side. Plato has Socrates say in the *Phaedo* that "doing" philosophy, that is, undergoing a philosophical education, is a kind of preparation for death. In Socrates' beautiful gallows speech, just prior to the hemlock, he comforts his companions—they being more distraught by his imminent martyrdom than he—with the

idea that there is nothing to fear in death if one has lived a contemplative life, one dwelling as much as possible amongst the Forms: "No
one may join the company of the gods who has not practiced philosophy and is not completely pure when he departs from life, no one but
the lover of learning" (82c). The lover of learning, the philosopher,
avoids worldly pain as well as pleasure, withdrawing from both as
far as possible, regarding each as merely "another nail to rivet the
soul to the body and to weld them together" (83d). Prefiguring Christian asceticism, one withdraws from change and decay, from imper-
fection and impurity, from the corporeal world itself, in favor of that
which is pristine and timeless and hence undying. To the extent one
can "participate" in the latter world, the world of Forms, one can
learn its laws and secrets, thereby gaining a kind of immortality-by-
association for oneself. One loses oneself in, say, mathematical theo-
rems; and that part of one so engaged escapes the fate of one's
corpse. The more one can lose oneself in the eternal realm, the less
one has to lose when death comes. However, insofar as one is preoccupied with sensual affairs, with food, drink, and sex, or with vanity,
moneymaking, and comfort, or with anger, sadness, joy, and laugh-
ter, one draws back from what is immortal and into the evanescent
and perishing:

> The soul of the philosopher achieves a calm from such emotions; it
> follows reason and ever stays with it contemplating the true, the divine,
> which is not the object of opinion. Nurtured by this, it believes that one
> should live in this manner as long as one is alive and, after death, arrive
> at what is akin and of the same kind, and escape from human ills.
> After such nurture there is no danger . . . that one should fear that, on
> parting from the body the soul would be scattered and dissipated by the
> winds and no longer be anything anywhere. (84b)

Thus the Pythagorean mystic-cum-Platonist aims not merely to discover the Truth but also to identify actively with it, to *become* it and
thereby live forever.

On the Platonic view, then, education's ultimate justification lies
in its securing of immortality for the lover of learning. Soul and body
being separate, education "turns" the soul out and frees it from its
bodily imprisonment (*Republic* 518b–d; *Phaedo*, passim.). The occupa-
tion of teaching flesh-and-blood human beings is for the most part
secondary; with one's eyes firmly fixed on the prize of immortality,
the Other-as-pupil is to be engaged only to the extent such pedagogical communion aids in deliverance unto the world of Forms. Analogous to the *Symposium*'s picture of "Platonic love," the beloved stu-

dent, a composite of body and soul, becomes in the end a means to a soulful, Truth-marrying end; one *ascends*, via an often near-consuming impassioned Eros, from the beautiful other to Beauty itself.[1] The other may indeed share this same end, but it is not to him or her that we look; Platonic teaching does not look *to* other human beings so much as it looks *with* them or, perhaps, *through* them.[2]

The other half of the unified Socratic vision, though, does look *to* the Other in order to find and preserve itself. This is the view of immortality animating my father's remark cited above: One lives on by influencing other human beings as a teacher, and then in the influence they, in turn, have on still others, and so on *ad infinitum*, like never-ending ripples in an infinite human pond. For the purposes of chronological consistency, I shall label this view "sophistic," not in Plato's derogatory sense, but, generically, as a reference to the professional teachers of fifth- and fourth-century B.C. Greece (see Kerferd, 1981). The Sophists *sold* their wisdom to others, mostly young male aristocrats who needed to "win friends and influence people" through rhetoric and other practical arts. Like all professionals, the Sophists collected fees, but what is central for present purposes is that, unlike Plato, and by virtue of their very trade, the Sophists tended to see the ultimate "payoff" of education as centered squarely in *human* affairs. Education is for skillful domestic management, acquiring and maintaining social status, and, most importantly, swaying hearts and minds in the law courts and in the Assembly.[3] As J. B. Bury (1975) writes:

> The institutions of a Greek democratic city presupposed in the average citizen the faculty of speaking in public, and for anyone who was ambitious for a political career it was indispensable. If a man was hauled into a law-court by his enemies and did not know how to speak, he was like an unarmed civilian attacked by soldiers. The power of expressing ideas clearly and in such a way as to persuade an audience was an art to be learned and taught. But it was not enough to gain command of a vocabulary; it was necessary to learn how to argue, and to exercise one's self in the discussion of political and ethical questions. There was a demand for higher education. (p. 241)

The Sophists, it must be remembered, were a mixed bag, representing a panoply of techniques, styles, and concerns, so one must be careful not to paint them with too broad a brush. But one generalization might withstand scrutiny, especially relative to the Platonists: Their main concern was by and large human and practical, focused as they were on preparing young men for civic life. Not that they were without ideals transcending utility, though. For example, as G. B. Kerferd notes, the pedagogical views of Protagoras, perhaps the subtlest of all the Sophists, may be summarized in Protagoras' statement that "Education does not sprout in the soul, unless one goes to a greater depth" (Diels & Kranz, 1952, 80B11). Indeed, by far the most influential educator of the day, a pupil of the famous Sophist Gorgias, was Isocrates, the rival—in many ways, successful—of Plato. In his important study, H. I. Marrou (1956) writes:

> On the whole it was Isocrates, not Plato, who educated fourth-century Greece and, subsequently the Hellenistic and Roman worlds; it was from Isocrates that, "as from a Trojan horse," there emerged all those teachers and men of culture, noble idealists, simple moralists, lovers of fine phrases, all those fluent voluble speakers, to whom classical antiquity owed both the qualities and the defects of its main cultural tradition. (p. 79)

But whatever depths sophistic pedagogy reached, it was first and foremost directed toward augmenting the success and influence of its charges in a thoroughly human world. The Sophists upheld the banner of "relevance to life" against, as they understood it, the Platonic school's obsession with "intellectual mastery of unimportant trifles" (Jaeger, 1944, p. 68).

Classical Greece, then, presents us with two *de facto* separable foci around which the ultimate purposes of education and, by extension, motivating reasons for teaching, may be articulated. The one looks "upward" to the star-lit divine: the Platonic shedding of this-worldly distractions pursuant to an epiphanous yet enduring identification with the *logos*, the articulation of truth—a yearning for a kind of immortality whose passageway is a glimpse at the structure and content of the cosmos. But the other ideal looks "downward" toward earth, to an educated *person* who can flourish him- or herself as well as garner prosperity—material, political, cultural, ethical—within and for the world of other human beings. This earthward-gazing sophistic ideal lives on through people and their associations, not sublimated in a disembodied reason.

Both ideals have a long subsequent history—most of which is far outside my present scope—where sometimes they run separately yet sometimes seem to converge and flow as one.

For present purposes it must suffice to say a bit about where things seem to stand at present, while gesturing toward a salutary reunification that seems, once again, possible for us to imagine. For both ideals are still powerfully with us today.

OUR CONTEMPORARY PLATONISTS

First, let us revisit Plato, this time in contemporary garb. The great tenor saxophonist Illinois Jacquet once said, "now I don't want to be around here forever, I just want to be a part of something that's gonna last forever" (Elgort, 1993). Implied in this statement about jazz, I think, is a concern for immortality not so distant from Plato's—which should not be surprising, after all, to find in a musician, music for Plato being an outflowing from a more primal celestial-mathematical harmony. Not wholly Platonic, of course (jazz music is a human creation, though what of the relations it expresses?), Jacquet is still articulating a rationale for doing what he does: At the end of the day it is worthwhile because it "links up" somehow with what is larger than his own immediate self, even larger than any individuals he has known or played with. In the above quotation he connects his legacy with something larger than himself or anyone in particular, that is, with *jazz music*. Posthumously, he was/is what he is by virtue of having been "a part of" that jazz music; his participation in it—could the language be any more Platonic?—defines his life's work, his artistic labors. At this momentary peak from which he surveys the course of his career, he does not choose to say that he sold a lot of records or made anybody's life better. He is *not* saying, as one often hears, "it all would've been worth it if I could've touched just one person," or anything of the kind. Not that he has *not* done this, though, or that it need be in any way distasteful to have done so. It is simply beside the point; the ultimate for this musician is just not to be found there. He is identifying himself with something larger, something altogether human, to be sure, but not for that reason *merely* human, something with its own life and times, maybe even its own death. In this sense, jazz is human, though not just human; and, as they say, the beat goes on.

Perhaps the most powerful embodiment of this Platonic kind of immortality is to be found in the research ethos animating the natural sciences (and emanating, owing to very this-worldly causes, from there to other "wanna be" areas of academic inquiry, including educational research). Need it be said that the scientific enterprise is in some important sense beyond the individuals it engages, beyond even historical epochs, nations, and cultures? This is not a point concerning the sociology of science or Thomas Kuhn. Maybe science as we know it is in some basic sense Western, patriarchal, trapped within some epistemic paradigm, or otherwise shot through with particularity, limitation, and human interest. Be that as it may, the present point concerns the ideals, the self-understanding of the activity, of its institutions and its practitioners, not its ontological status. The Nobel Prize–winning physicist Steven Weinberg (1993) is not *merely* naive when he writes, "It certainly feels to me that we are discovering something real in physics, something that is what it is without any regard to the social or historical conditions that allowed us to discover it" (p. 188). Embarrassing as it may be to the luxury box-seat observers of scientific research, from the players themselves, like Weinberg, slips the voice of the "Real."

In this sense I wager that we are still Greek to the following extent: Imagine there were no short- or long-term "real-world" pay-offs to knowing the way the universe is structured, nothing one could make or do as a result. For that reason would we no longer want to *know*? A colleague of mine tells of a mathematician years ago at the Institute for Advanced Study at Princeton who on occasion could be heard, as he sat by himself in his office late at night, weeping at the beauty of a mathematical proof. Is this just a *silly* man? One gone insane? Hardly. This is a man better described as having a foothold in an immortal realm, halfway between human beings and the gods. So says the Platonist in our scientists. These are the ones whose motivation (admittedly, all too rare) lies in reaching for what is apart from the day-to-day. This is why, alone with a scratch sheet for numbers and formulae, a mathematician can shed the wondering, wonderful tears of a child.[4] Again, Weinberg: "It is when we study truly fundamental problems that we expect to find beautiful answers" (ibid., p. 163).

Buried somewhere far beneath the grant-getting, the contracts, the everydayness, the engineering applications, and the sociology of scientific research, there lies a motivating purity, one captured in that solitary yet singularly unlonely weeping. This is an unpopularly uncynical position, I realize. It assumes a distinction—far beyond my present scope to defend—between science and technology, as well as one between science and politics, each in broad senses. (If our scientists no longer weep, perhaps this means that we no longer have scientists.) The point for now is that there is a skyward Platonic gaze that has motivated scientific research in our culture and, here and there, still seems to do so. Consider the following from Albert Einstein:

I believe with Schopenhauer that one of the strongest motives that leads men to art and science is escape from everyday life with its painful crudity and hopeless dreariness, from the fetters of one's own ever-shifting desires. A finely tempered nature longs to escape from personal life into the world of objective perception and thought; this desire may be compared with the townsman's irresistible longing to escape from his noisy, cramped surroundings into the high mountains, where the eye ranges freely through the still, pure air and fondly traces out the restful contours apparently built for eternity. (Quoted in Hoffmann, 1972, p. 221)[5]

Plato could not have said it better himself.

On these understandings, teaching is worthwhile because it continues and extends a noetic search for the *cosmos*, for the truth about the universe, not because it creates for oneself new and fashionable -isms or a circle of devotees (though it may in fact do this). Every research paper's footnote becomes swept up in the quest, dragging in tow the efforts of precursors both famous and obscure. In this sense, Isaac Newton, regardless of how he is surpassed by relativity and quantum mechanics, is never dead and buried but is living in deathless nurturance of an undertaking that is "gonna last forever." Even as he dismantles the Newtonian worldview, Einstein pauses in his notes, offering an apologia across the centuries: "Enough of this. Newton forgive me. You found the only way that, in your day, was at all possible for a man of the highest powers of intellect and creativity. The concepts that you created still dominate the way we think in physics, although we now know that they must be replaced by others farther removed from the sphere of immediate experience if we want to try for a more profound understanding of the way things are interrelated" (ibid., pp. 247–248).

The beat goes on here, too.

OUR CONTEMPORARY SOPHISTS

However powerful this Platonism of the scientist, it is the sophistic kind of immortality that is far more common in society at large, particularly among schoolteachers, usually so far removed from "advancing the frontiers of knowledge," from the research ideal, but all the closer to the actual human beings for whom they care and whom they bring along. This is an ideal that binds together parents, educators, and lawmakers—that of "making the world a better place," where "world" is understood as a *populated* one. How many tales are told of the Great Teacher—the Master, the Mentor, Mom and Dad—without whom the speaker would not be here today? How much ink has been spilled, how many trees felled, to supply us with such literature (itself an apparently undying phenomenon)? But however hackneyed the literary form, how many teachers can deny their desire to be that Great Teacher, at least once, or twice, or once in a while? Here it makes sense to say, as it does not for Illinois Jacquet or for Albert Einstein, "if I can reach just one person it will all have been worth it." The smallest pebble creates ripples on the water's surface just as surely as the boulder. One may of course speak of a teacher as having "more" or "less" influence, but talk of quantity seems out of place here. Does "reaching" ten children—whatever that may in the end mean—make your teaching career twice as worthwhile as that of the teacher who has reached five? Such talk is inappropriate because each case is irreducibly unique; the deep and lasting influence one has defies that kind of measurement. From the perspective of eternity, no one can be *twice* as immortal as someone else. One either is or is not.

Listening to the voices of committed teachers themselves, one so often hears the earthward call of the Other-as-human-being, of children and other students. Louise, a second-grade teacher in the New York suburbs, says to an interviewer, "I think the biggest reward [of my job] is watching the light bulb turn on in somebody's head. You try five or six approaches to get an idea across, and all of a sudden the child says, 'Oh, you mean . . . ' and you say, 'Thank you, God. Yes, that is what I mean.'" Louise's colleague Ann adds, "I agree. Also to watch them grow and see the people they have become by June . . . " (Dichter, 1989, p. 218). A suburban high school English teacher from the Los Angeles area, Brenda Ring, expands upon Ann and Louise's sentiment: "If I can make kids enjoy English, I am happy. I've found my niche in life with teaching . . . I feel good about what I do. I enjoy 30 different personalities each hour. I see kids feel good about things they do. I can get kids to respond. I have a lot of leeway with what I can do in class. It stirs my creativity to come up with assignments. Because I teach English, I get the kids to write journals and so I really get to know them" (Yee, 1990, p. 218). The challenge here for her, that is, the source of Ring's classroom creativity, is located in the particularities of each child, responding to a chorus (perhaps sometimes a cacophony!) of calls earthward. It should be noted, too, that this call may be in its own way as intellectually demanding as any other human activity could possibly be—finding what resonates with an individual may call for the most subtle cleverness—but it is an effort whose terminus is always a *person*, not a structure, a landscape, a concept, or a proof.

If there is a heart to teaching, this must be close to it. In her study of teaching as a career, Sylvia Yee (1990) describes a group she calls "good-fit stayers," teachers whose outlook and abilities mesh well with the career of teaching's demands and who are in addition motivated to persevere in it. Good-fit stayers on the whole love what they are doing and want to keep doing it. More often than not they cannot imagine anything they would rather do than teach. Yee finds that this group seems drawn to teaching for something like teaching's sake, for reasons intrinsic to the activity itself (as opposed to extrinsic rewards such as salary or vacation time). She writes:

> Comments such as "my main enjoyment is contact with kids" or "I love to watch the excitement of their learning" capture these teachers' positive attitudes about their work. Good-fit teachers, moreover, typically are uninterested in administrative work because they are unwilling to lose touch with the students. These teachers are also more apt to say such things as "I love my students" or "the kids are great" and to view their students as a source of fun, stimulation, and appreciation. (p. 95)

Moreover, as Yee argues, such teachers derive further sustenance from proof that they are "making a difference" in their students' lives; their motivation is reinforced when they are convinced of their own efficacy in making that difference. In fact, "teachers for whom intrinsic rewards from classroom work are plentiful are usually motivated to seek professional growth and to spend more time and effort in the classroom—behavior that reinforces or further stimulates self-efficacy," whereas teachers who "do not experience their work with students as a major inducement to stay or to contribute their best efforts . . . emphasize extrinsic sources of reward as their reasons to stay; they are also more likely to withhold personal contributions by leaving, or, worse, by settling into on-the-job retirement" (ibid., p. 109).

Clearly, the stakes concerning where a teacher's motivation lies are high. This is not of course to suggest that there are no additional valid reasons to sustain a teaching career. (Various nonclassroom activities associated with professional development, as Yee notes, come to mind.) But it is to say that teaching makes the most moral—and motivational—sense when the human beings implicated in the enterprise are understood as its primary focus. One would think this commonsensical, were it not for perspectives that attempt to remove the spotlight from the children themselves and place it on, say, some national economic scheme or some political, cultural, or religious agenda. From what I am calling the earthward perspective, these latter represent so many flights from the moral core of a teacher's efforts, the concrete Other. "As a teacher, I am, first, one-caring" as Nel Noddings (1984) puts it; a teacher who cares is always mindful that his or her student "must be aware that for me he is more important, more valuable than the subject" (pp. 174, 176). And if Yee and the others are correct, the teacher's own livelihood (in the literal sense of "vitality") depends upon as much. A master's degree student of my own, an elementary school teacher in downstate Illinois, Cathy Bissoondial (1993), brings the threads of the preceding discussion together with an unassuming elegance (the reader will permit me a bit of teacherly pride in her words!), as she writes in a journal entry:

> I guess what I'm trying to say is that I don't know what the purpose of education is or, maybe more accurately, whose notion is correct. I can only speak to what I try to instill in students as they are members of my class for one short year. What influences do I have? What difference do I make? Can I be all things to all people? Absolutely not. But which call do I answer? Economy's? Democracy's? Society's? Or is there a small voice crying softly in the corner which I haven't heard over the din of the others? Whose utterance is it? Perhaps it is my own. . . .

It is appropriate to ask, as Cathy implicitly does, whether this voice of the Other is so deep within the Other that, paradoxically, it is in some sense "my own"? Does teaching call forth some human substratum, illuminate some living nexus? How else could I, the teacher, standing over "here," also be "there"? How else could it be that the call of the Other must in some sense be heard in order to teach? Spatial and temporal boundaries around my students and me begin to erode.

This is even clearer when we reverse directional frames and look at the teacher-as-carer's repository, the student him- or herself. In ourselves, if we look hard enough, we often see the ghosts of teachers past, as has often been noted. Thomas Robinson and Walter Brower (1982) ask us to ask ourselves, "What teacher or teachers live on, with earned immortality, in me?," as they reflect upon their own mourning for the passing of a "respected teacher friend" (p. 714). Like most funerals, the one they describe was sad. Yet it was not on balance a sorrowful affair, much somberness being dissipated as several students began to voice their remembrances of their erstwhile teacher. Consider just a few of the encomia heard that day:

> Each week, in our ninth-grade English class, he had us write a composition. I wrote a whole novel, a chapter each week. I still have it. I reread it several days ago, when I learned of his serious illness. He made me a lover of the written word. . . . He was the chief influence in my going to college. When he was a high school teacher, he invited my parents and me to his home to discuss the possibility of college for me. He persuaded them to send me and even helped me get scholarship help. . . . He taught me to love reading. . . . It's because of him that I became our town library's best customer. . . . All I can say about him can be summed up in this statement . . . I wanted to be like him. He was both my textbook and my model. Because of him I became a principal, and I'm now a high school principal in Pennsylvania. . . . [A woman who is now a professor of literature added that] I am what I am professionally because that man, in a junior high school, insisted that each graduating class have a class poet who would prepare a commemorative commencement poem. I was chosen for my class. I was later my college class poet. In the ninth grade, because of him, the firm foundation of my life was laid. (p. 714)

Could a teacher ask for more than pedagogical progeny like these? Like a variation on the Native American myth in which a powerful person's soul is taken by a woman in the form of a crow, here we have a flock of crows, some ducking, some soaring, some helping others along, and some, in their own way, signaling to still others— perhaps to a straggler or an entire and as yet grounded flock—to come and fly alongside, behind, or ahead.

An excursus into the realm of myth is in no way inappropriate here, given that the nature of a teacher's influence often enough resists the kind of measurement a positivist would require. Philip Jackson (1992), for example, argues that most adults are probably scarcely able to name the teachers who influenced them, let alone pinpoint exactly who they are (though there are of course exceptions here and there). But this form of selective amnesia hardly diminishes those forgotten influences' significance. For Jackson, only an excessive focus upon *knowing* those influences' precise provenances would lead to such a conclusion; he suggests we take a lesson from philosophical skepticism and just learn to *accept* some things. One is grateful to a teacher, even if one never knows precisely for what.

Even supposing, *per impossibile*, one were able to establish a chart, perhaps some "influence tree" with all its many branches, one's self-understanding in this area still might not be advanced a great deal. One of my own branches would certainly be my eighth-grade algebra teacher, Mrs. Lewis. (My account draws from and happens to run parallel in many respects to Jackson's memorable description of his own algebra teacher, "Mrs. Henzi.") But what exactly *was* it about her that was so influential? It is not at all clear that I would ever be able to determine it precisely. Candidates I can imagine seem inevitably lacking somehow: solving quadratic equations, being made to do more homework than I ever thought humanly possible, coming to terms with public at-the-blackboard admissions of fallibility (oh, so many of those!), the "seriousness" with which we learned to approach the subject matter (to again borrow from Jackson's "Mrs. Henzi"), the badge of intellectual and fortitudinal honor that being a veteran of her class entitled one to wear throughout junior high and beyond, and so on. Can I say with any certainty that any one of these is "it," or even that I've identified "the two" or "the three" things for which I'm most indebted? Considering them all, it begins to take on the appearance of the magician's trick of pulling scarves out of a hat: I keep pulling out more and more "influences," yet while I do still more influences appear. Soon the whole enterprise of charting influences grows murkier and murkier. One begins to suspect that there exists an underground teeming multitude of teacherly influences, so many of them far beneath our accustomed cognitive radar scope. And although a great many such bonds may not be accessible to cognition, although they may never be "known" in that narrow sense, they may, to paraphrase Dewey, nonetheless be *had*. I may even suffer the delusion of thinking I am "self-taught," yet my illness of positivism reduces my obligation to those unnamed influential others not one whit.

THE PROBLEM OF EGOISM

Yet however enmeshed all of us may be in this relational and multidirectional web of influences, there are still serious moral issues to which the teacher-as-immortal must attend. More specifically, there are warranted worries about this picture of immortality through teaching that I have been building—mostly because it appears to smack of an egoism unseemly in a truly caring and hence Other-directed teacher. In the extreme, in fact, it seems positively vampirish: The morbidly self-centered teacher searches for promising victims in whom his or her "influence" can survive. Even worse, as such a teacher, I may start to view my students as so many opportunities to carbon-copy myself—my classroom a nightmarish (or maybe merely comical) sort of zomboid assembly line. A variation might be a teacherly analogue to the "Little League parent," who imposes his or her own dreams and lost opportunities onto the student, running roughshod over the individuality—not to mention the mental health—of the emotionally trapped child. "I want to give you what I never had" so often has its price.

A final worry lies in the idea of having influence *as such*, as opposed to having an *educative* influence. Recall the notorious English teacher, Mr. Ostrowski, from *The Autobiography of Malcolm X* (Malcolm X, 1965) who told young Malcolm Little that, despite his demonstrated intellectual talents, he should lower his sights from law school to a more manual trade like carpentry, owing to his race. ("But you've got to be realistic about being a nigger. A lawyer—that's no realistic goal for a nigger" [p. 36].) This teacher surely "lives on" posthumously. But in that way so do not only Mr. Ostrowski (a "well-meaning" bigot, to be sure), but also Adolf Hitler and the Waco, Texas, Branch Davidian cult leader David Koresh.

Bad guys have their kind of immortality, too. But is this what an educator is after? Plain notoriety? This cannot be so, for mere infamy, as I shall make clearer below, is far too lonely a proposition for a teacher. What is needed here is immortality *as an educator*, an (after)-life with living meaning. The notion of "influence" must be modified accordingly somehow.

Ironically, the antidote to egoism and manipulation (both of which one might call, with Zygmunt Bauman [1992], "immortality strategies") is to be found in that same Platonic skyward gaze that tends to appear so coldly impersonal to the caringly earthbound teacher. For such abuses are prevented precisely by one who cares for the *logos*, by one who is disposed toward Truth-seeking, even against immediate self-interest. Here, literally, is a teacher "beyond influence," one dedicated above all to ushering the student into some arena of human understanding, not one recruiting acolytes for oneself or for some "cause." Paradoxically, you can find yourself in your pupil precisely by refusing to let her find herself in *you*, admonishing her, as would Nietzsche's Zarathustra, "One repays a teacher badly if one always remains nothing but a pupil. And why do you not want to pluck at my wreath?" (Nietzsche, 1892/1954, p. 78). In this sense, the "truthful" teacher is *ipso facto* readied for the dissolution of the ego; he does not pretend to possess impossible Truths, but rather allows himself to be possessed of the intellectual virtue of Socratic ignorance—which one must realize is consistent with a "will to truth," to adopt Nietzsche's phrase—where the search never culminates in dogmatic and restful possession, but only in still further dogged and restive pursuit. If my aim is to teach what is true, I am at once placed beyond the more mundane egoistic forms of corruption mentioned above. Plato understands this well when he ensures that in his *Republic* the Guardians of the state are lovers of learning first and rulers only reluctantly, pulled by the collar as they must be from their turn at the pipe in their preferred opium den of philosophizing (540b–e). As always, there is a grain of insight in even the most outrageous Platonic proposal.

Thus the egoistic perversion of immortality through one's students is held in check by an allegiance to something beyond the teacher–student dyad, something to which both sets of eyes must be turned. Conversely, however, the earthward glance that sees teaching as ensconced in human affairs countervails just as critically against *its* opposite—the notion that education culminates in an attachment to some pristine, non-human Truth-in-Itself. The difficulty at this extreme is that sublimating oneself to the search for universal truths is no longer necessarily harmless, as the figure of the atomic physicist warns us so eloquently. The scientist-cum-technologist tinkering with irresistible brain puzzles may be tinkering at the same time with a great deal else (e.g., human lives, the biosphere). Thus our latter-day scientific Platonists, to continue with this convenient example, find themselves encumbered inescapably by responsibilities of a *social* nature, by duties tethering them back to an all-too-human world, even as cognition strains to break free of such associative bonds. The physicist Edward Teller's statement that "it is *not* the scientist's job to determine whether a hydrogen bomb should be constructed, whether it should be used, or how it should be used" (Quoted in Boyer, 1985, p. 342) sounds less and less convincing in a world poised for high-tech annihilation as our post–Cold War world still is.

To guard against disaster, then, the teacher-learner of science—even at the most rarefied levels of research—must attend to the voices of other human beings. What are the consequences of my research? How am I implicated? Should I be? Such questions strike uncomfortably near the heart of Platonism as a guide to pedagogy, and the asking of them illustrates the limits to Plato's other-worldly extreme, an obsession that can now be mobilized to destroy its own conditions for existence in a Strangelovian push of the button. How much "Truth" can we uncover if we blow up the planet, or let it die a slow toxic death from our plastic abundance? It should be remembered that Plato never satisfactorily answers the following questions: After escaping out onto the sunlit surface, why should I return to the shadowy all-too-human cave? Why not stay outside among the Forms? Why should I care to go back? What obliges me to share my learning, to teach? Without a preexisting bond with other human beings, such questions can have no answer, and Plato's assumption that the teacher should return to the cave merely presupposes rather than argues for such intersubjective ties.[6] As Bernard Williams (1972) has noted, one cannot *argue* a person into caring for someone else. All one can hope is to render the human ties more perspicuous; if they are not there—somewhere—all is pathologically lost (p. 10).

Two equally pernicious forms of egoism, then, are to be avoided in this context: what one might call the "egoism of obliviousness" that tempts the scientist-Platonist, along with the "egoism of monomania" that may corrupt the human-centered teacher. The pedagogical challenge here is to develop an ability to play both extremes off of one another somehow and thus to avoid falling headlong into either one of them—something of a delicate moral tightrope act. Sophistic pedagogy's earthward gaze in this way grounds the moral voice that calls the educator back from the brink of Platonic indifference, just as a dose of Platonism wards off egoism and manipulation from the overly human-centered teacher. Yet this criss-crossing of motivation is not at all a simple matter. On the contrary, it will require daily, perhaps hourly, negotiation and renegotiation in response to the exigencies of practice. As a teacher, one can be corrupted from many directions: subject, child, and self may center as well as decenter, depending on the situation. One might say that teaching is by nature a perpetually corruptible business, suitable only for those who do not mind getting their hands a little dirty, for those whose moral compass continues to operate well even under conditions of extreme ambiguity, frustration, and "no-win" situations. Required is the artistry, a sort of Aristotelian phronetic "sense," not only of how to avoid the extremes, but also how to use them to maintain the sweet spot at the center, adjusting the tension from each end as need be.

Does my caring ever cloud my vision as to what is true? Can I lie to a student if it increases his or her self-esteem, for example? (What warrants, in other words, our faith that truth can never be painful and stunting?) And on the other hand, is my interest in the subject matter—in my own research perhaps—occluding its human context? What of my cognitive titillation, not to mention my career advancement, if it makes no difference to human lives, or if it somehow contributes to making them worse? These are questions educator-immortals must face day in and day out if they are to be such.

TOWARD AN EQUILIBRIUM

Although there are no easy answers, no blueprint for achieving the equilibrium of immortality just outlined, there is an ancient model reemerging among certain contemporary educators that may well achieve a great deal toward reconciling the two extremes. The first place to look for clues is back at the beginning of the story I have told, back to Socrates as he appears in Plato's early "Socratic" dialogues— a Socrates most scholars agree is more *Socrates* than the Platonic mouthpiece he becomes in Plato's later writings (e.g., *The Republic*, as noted in Vlastos, 1990). As in Platonic monologue, in the Socratic dialectic, the Truth is always the end-in-view of a discussion; at stake is typically an answer to the question "What is X?" (e.g., piety, courage, virtue). Strangely, though, positive answers are rarely if ever given. For example, the *Euthyphro*, an investigation of piety, ends merely with a call for further investigation into piety (15d), and in the *Meno*, the grand finale posits the unsatisfying "conclusion" that virtue can be neither taught nor learned in the usual way, but "appears to be present in those of us who may possess it as a gift from the Gods" (100b).

What are we to make, in the present context, of these examples of the famous Socratic profession of ignorance? Two things at least: First, though the search for Truth is a noble one, requiring all sorts of attendant virtues, perhaps even a religious zeal as in the case of Socrates himself, only a fool would ever claim to have it in final form. Second, and most important for present purposes, *one can only take sincere aim at that ever-elusive Truth via other similarly inquiring human beings, through dialogue.* One cannot do it alone. But neither can one do it with just any others. One needs *learners* in the truest sense, as opposed to debate team antagonists who want to "win" an argument and come off looking to others as if they have done so. Needless to say, dialogue is also foreclosed when an interlocutor aims merely to convince the other of a preconceived verity, as in the case of an interrogation, a "drill-and-practice" computer program, or political "consciousness raising." These things may sometimes be worth-while, even necessary, but why confuse them with dialogue in this larger sense, the heart and soul of education?

In true dialogue, teacher and learner are irrevocably human, but somehow also more than human, driven along as they are by an intertwining of skyward and earthward gazes. In H.-G. Gadamer's (1976) philosophical hermeneutics—one of the main loci for the renewed interest in dialogue in education—this dual movement is likened to the playing of a game that, as a game does, depends on its players but is also larger than any one of those players' sum (p. 66). Education, with its teacher-learners, is a game of this sort, with all the attendant aporias: We play it. Or does it play us? We "get it"? Or does it get us? This ambiguity must be preserved lest the preconditions for dialogue in the Socratic sense be lost. Teacher and student care for one another by *taking care* to allow the arising of the subject matter itself—the *logos*—that is to be disclosed in their interaction. As Shaun Gallagher (1992) puts it, "the subject matter itself, however, not the teacher, is the thing that must elicit interest and demand effort in the form of a question" (p. 165). In any given case, much work may need to be done to create the material conditions for educational experience in this sense. For the teacher, more caring, nurturing, legislature-lobbying, picketing, and the like—in short, more blood, sweat, and tears than one can tell—may need to be accomplished first or concurrent with the activity for the sake of which those things are done. But all the while, the dual allegiances of teaching, to something like truth and to each other, must be held in balance. William Ayers (1993) captures well this duality, this equipoise:

> The work of a teacher—exhausting, complex, idiosyncratic, never twice the same—is, at its heart, an intellectual and ethical enterprise. Teaching is the vocation of vocations, a calling that shepherds a multitude of other callings. It is an activity that is intensely practical and yet transcendent, brutally matter-of-fact, and yet fundamentally a creative act. (p. 127)

Who or what it is that creates "in"education, however (as I think Ayers would agree), is neither just a teacher nor just a student, but rather, at once, both of them and more than both. It is in this "more than" that immortality resides. "Education writ large," Jackson (1992) writes, "is not mine alone. We all share it, students, parents, citizens at large, even teachers themselves—indeed maybe teachers more than others, who knows?" (p. 18). The teacher-as-immortal is neither "over here" nor "up there" but is cross-stitched into a mindful fabric that binds us, warms us from the cold, and, eventually, serves for all of us teacher-learners as our burial shroud. Education is neither "mine" nor "yours," but both of us may *become* it.

A suitable parable with which to conclude this opening chapter may be found, appropriately enough, in the story of the original mentor, Mentor, the character in Homer's *Odyssey*, that same Mentor who plaintively counsels: "Yet not even the Gods can ward off from a man they love/The death that is common to all at whatever time/ The ruinous fate of all-sorrowful death seizes him" (III, 236–238). Mentor leads the son Telemachos in his search for Odysseus his long-lost father. Yet in doing so Mentor does not speak in his own voice. His role is to serve as a mouthpiece for Pallas Athene, goddess of wisdom and the lost father's guardian. Athene chooses to take on the visage and voice of Mentor as she guides the young searcher Telemachos. A wise learner, Telemachos allows her. Wisdom thus speaks *through* Mentor, not *from* him, and so is heard; Mentor's proper role is to vanish into wisdom for the sake of wisdom's pupil, as the pupil searches for his past and for his future. So must die the teacher in order to live. And thus in turn rehearses the learner for "the death that is common to all."

CHAPTER 2

Immortality Alone

A feeling of pleasure overcame me. I realized that what I embody, the principle of life, cannot be destroyed. It is written into the cosmic code, the order of the universe. As I continued to fall in the dark void, embraced by the vault of the heavens, I sang to the beauty of the stars and made my peace with the darkness.

—Heinz Pagels (1982)

DEATH'S DISTANCE AND RETURN

Teaching seems at first so much more about life than about death. And viewed from a certain angle, this is undoubtedly so. But such presentiments beg an important question, namely, the neat and clean separation between life and death themselves. This is indeed the reigning way we have come to see the two: as opposites that exclude one another. Wherever one is, the other cannot be, as fire melts ice and good repels evil. None other than Plato himself inaugurates the distinction in the *Phaedo*:

Socrates: Do you not say that to be dead is the opposite of being alive?
Cebes: I do.
S: And they come to be from one another?
C: Yes.
S: What comes to be from being alive?
C: Being dead.
S: And what comes to be from being dead?
C: One must agree that it is being alive.
S: Then, Cebes, living creatures and things come to be from the dead?
C: So it appears.
S: Then our souls exist in the underworld.
C: That seems likely. (*Phaedo* 71d–e)

Just as being asleep and being awake "come from one another," one driving the other out in order to be present, life and death coexist, but as opposites. The "proof" from opposites is one of Plato's arguments—probably the weakest—for the immortality of the soul.[1] Suffice it to say that it clearly begs the question at issue by assuming what it sets out to prove, namely, the persistence of the soul or subject.[2] Whatever the flaws in Plato's argument, though, the image he presents has triumphed (in the West at least), albeit gradually.

Burial practices of the classical period seem to indicate, however, that dying was not always understood as a clash of opposites. Plato's own contemporaries apparently held views significantly different from his, not distinguishing so sharply between the living and the dead. Robert Garland (1985) points out that in ancient Greece, death was generally understood not so much as an instantaneous event but rather a process that required "strenuous action on the part of the survivors in order to be successfully terminated" (p. 13). Plato breaks from this tradition by introducing the theme that death is more like a struggle in which the soul (*psuchē*) is released from the body, foreshadowing the later Christian idea of the death struggle (*psuchorrhagema*). (In Homer, for example, out of some 240 deaths that are depicted, only 4 are described in terms of the soul departing—and these four are persons of heroic status, that is, "special cases" [ibid., p. 18].) Neither were the ancient Greeks obsessed with what one might call the "otherness" of death, its ghoulishness. There was no morbid fascination, for example, with rotting corpses, skeletons, and such that haunted the late medieval Christian mind and its ever-present motif of *memento mori* (usually a skull or cadaver tucked away in the corner of an artist's depiction of what might otherwise be a festive scene). The ancient Greeks never quite accepted the parting of the soul and the body; the "shades" in Hades are never quite what they were while alive and are usually quite pathetic figures with little power. For the most part, as Emily Vermeule (1979) summarizes, "their myths had the gates of heaven or the great sky closed against mortals" (pp. 118–122, 136).

Our Judeo-Christian heritage may indeed have opened the gates of heaven for us, but this has come at the cost of a gradual distancing of the living from death. Death becomes something essentially alien to ourselves, our *true* selves, our eternal souls. We shove death away in so many ways.

I remember as a child attending my grandfather's funeral, which was conducted more or less according to Jewish custom. Now Jewish funerals are more or less earthbound affairs. I do not think any of us even thought in terms of souls, let alone "the hereafter," at least explicitly.[3] Neither was the corpse an object of much attention: There is no barbaric (most any Jew would describe it thus) embalming and displaying of the corpse, for example. Indeed, I remember very well my mother and her sister being asked to throw the first, heartbreaking shovel of dirt onto the newly interred coffin to symbolize the finality of the burial. (My mother could not bring herself to do it.) Yet I remember also how, at the "condolence meal" afterwards, the chief mourners (the closest kin, my mother and aunt) were actually seated lower to the ground than the less-than-chief mourners (myself included), as a reminder of their closeness to the deceased, a scene that in any other context might look comical. But for me what most comes back to mind is waiting in line in front of my aunt and uncle's small house after returning from the burial and then one by one washing our hands on the front porch before entering. This was, of course, but a ceremonial washing: just water from some nice pitcher and a towel. But the message of this particular ritual was patently clear to me, whatever its theological provenance: We were washing our hands of the dead and returning to a home, a place for the living.

As I said, Judaism as I have known it seems to me relatively earthy and practical about such matters. The overall idea behind the funeral, as I recall my mother and cousins (half) joking, was to get the whole thing over with as quickly as possible and get on with your life.[4] By contrast, I cannot even imagine what one would go through at a traditional Catholic funeral, with your loved one in an open casket, dressed up and perfumed, with talk of the dearly departed up in heaven (or maybe feared in that other place), looking down on things or whatever the dead are supposed to do a few days after dying—perhaps necessitating a wakeful vigilance as protection for the soul or to make sure for three days that the dead are really dead, as was the ancient custom (Paxton, 1990, pp. 21–22).

Ultimately, perhaps the open-casket display shows a healthier relationship with death—less fearful, less traumatized by the idea of a corpse. I do not know. But what does seem to me true is that both religions have powerful ways in which to distance themselves from the dead. The Jews get it over with quickly and relatively decisively, "washing their hands" of it, whereas the Catholics prolong the whole affair as long as they can, keeping the corpse around and praying to and for the still-and-always-living individual soul of the deceased.

Consider how, in historical context, this distancing has been the trend. Philippe Ariès, the preeminent historian of European death, has argued that from around the fifth to the eighteenth centuries, the living and the dead were not so separated, physically and imagistically, as they were to become subsequently. During this period, "the dead ceased to frighten the living, and the two groups coexisted in the same places and behind the same walls" (Ariès, 1981, p. 30). After the eighteenth century or so, burial sites became more circumscribed and detached from everyday life. The cemetery became a much more singular place, cordoned off from the quotidian. But according to Ariès, what has resulted from our attempts to put death at arm's length is precisely the opposite of what it might be thought we were setting out to achieve. We have gone from a situation in which death was "tamed," that is, more familiar, closer yet also somewhat desensitized (one thinks of the appalling mortality rates during the "tame" period) to the more recent situation in which death has become "wild," an object of fascinating horror, or something just plain odd, a case in point being the "peculiar embarrassment felt by the living in the presence of dying people," as the sociologist Norbert Elias (1985) observes (p. 23). Death becomes an indeterminate zone where ritual now breaks down; as a result of our distancing efforts, Elias adds, "dying is at present a largely unformed situation, a blank area on the social map" (ibid., p. 28).

One of the most important aspects of this distancing of death, and hence the creating of the possibility of its becoming wild in Ariès's sense, has been its medicalization—even pathologization—a fate dying now shares with many other basic processes, such as childbirth. Barring something out of the ordinary, most of us these days can expect to die alone in a hospital bed, just as most mothers can now enjoy being "spectators" at their own baby's birth (as a physician acquaintance once ecstatically and unironically declaimed to me). This process seems to follow the rough pattern of something like the so-called dialectic of enlightenment as laid out by the Frankfurt School theorists Max Horkheimer and Theodore Adorno. Characteristic of our times, they hold, is an "instrumental rationality," wherein we focus with greater and greater intensity on perfecting the means of our activity, our techniques, while we concomitantly lose our ability to consider the ends of that same activity. This gives us a great and liberating technical proficiency at curing disease, producing food, reducing mortality rates from childbirth, and so forth. But our dangerously myopic lack of attention to the ends of that ever-increasing proficiency can be alienating, irrational, and dangerous. Horkheimer (1974) writes: "Reason is calculative; it can assess truths of fact and mathematical relations but nothing more. In the realm of practice it can speak only of means. About ends it must be silent" (p. 57). As the Enlightenment's dialectic springs back from the latest can-do triumph, we find that our technical excellence can also be deployed in the service of atom bombs and concentration camps. Horkheimer and Adorno's prototype is Odysseus, that same father who helped peacefully to close the first chapter, whose cleverness, craft, and skill culminate in the orgiastic, bloody slaughter of his long-faithful Penelope's suitors.[5] It is almost as if a cruel joke has been perpetrated on Western culture: We get better and better at getting there, only to find that we have lost control over where we are headed.

One might certainly question whether Horkheimer and Adorno's deep cultural pessimism is warranted, at least as a consummate diagnosis of modernity as a whole (for example, the implausible hyperbole of blaming modernity in general for the Nazis).[6] But I would suggest that at least in the overlapping spheres that are here my primary concern—mortality and education—the instrumental rationality motif is not without its explanatory power. Its workings can be subtle, though, and one must be attentive to notice them. Consider again the medicalization of death and what is involved there. What one finds is that our very experience of our own mortality has flown away from us and has thus, in Ariès's paradoxical sense, becomes wild and ever-wilder as we increase our attempts to sanitize and otherwise tame it. In Bauman's (1992) words, we tend to deal with our collective death anxiety by hygenically "putting mortality in an institutional and mental confinement and keeping it there" (p. 154).

What do we know about death? When I was 8 years old, I proclaimed to my incredulous year-younger sister that we—she or I— could die at any time. Not that either of us is likely to drop dead right away, but it is *possible* that we could. Who knows? Some rapid-killing disease could strike, the roof could cave in, an errant bomb from the local military base could drop. These are the types of things I was thinking of. In fact, I (to her ears) morbidly went on: I bet many people die sort of "out of the blue," not expecting it at all. You're skipping down the garden path one day feeling the warmth of the sun and then—bam!—for whatever reason, you're dead. But she turned to me and said I was wrong; it was impossible. Not for *us* at least. We are just children; we do not *die*.

Now I was the incredulous one: I did not see why it should even be controversial. I was not saying we were *going* to die in the next few moments or that it was even likely, though both of us know—don't we?—that we will eventually, though that hardly matters now: By then we will be different creatures altogether, *old* ones for goodness sake. I was just talking about the logical possibility of its happening (though, of course, I did not put it in those terms then). So how could my sister be so dense, I wondered? Maybe it's because she is just 7. Not likely, though: She was there, after all, when we both cried time and time again when Mother got to the part in *Charlotte's Web* (White, 1952) when Wilbur the pig thought he was about to get slaughtered—just a warm-up, mind you, for the real crying occasioned when the self-sacrificing spider Charlotte died her "natural" death. We did weep about *something* then, something we understood somehow. Didn't we?[7]

At the risk of overdignifying my childhood obsessions, I think the "argument" between my sister and me might be viewed as something much larger than the two of us, as a clash between two worlds, two vastly different ways of understanding our own mortality. It seems to me that my 8-year-old self was the more "rational" of the two of us, and not just because it is, after all, physically possible that anyone could die for some reason at any moment. I mean in the much deeper sense of the way in which my very conceiving of the notion of death was framed. Despite what I may have been saying on the surface, I was not really thinking about death as a possibility *for me*. I was making the quick and easy analogical inference, a sort of quasi-syllogism, that (1) People die all of the time, many of them when they are not expecting it; (2) My sister and I are persons just like those others; therefore (3) We could die when we were not expecting it, whenever (including now). Who could find fault with such impeccable logic? Clearly I was right. So precocious was I, I "knew" all about death. Right?

To sight this problem more clearly, I will enlist the aid of the German philosopher Martin Heidegger, in many ways an anti-Enlightenment thinker, whose ideas about mortality (and a great many other things) have been so vastly influential—and controversial—throughout this century. One of Heidegger's central concepts is what he called the "ontological difference" between Being (note the honorific capital "B") and entities. In a nutshell, for Heidegger, the grand story of Western metaphysics since Plato has been a forced march away from the more primal understanding of Being hinted at in the fragments of the earliest Greek philosophers, the pre-Socratics. Along the way of this march, we have come to understand the world—in our most basic thought-patterns—as populated by entities: discrete things that as such await our use, control, and domination.

The ancients, by contrast, viewed the world as very much alive, as animated in some basic way (witness pretechnological cultural practices such as totemism and animism); "living" and "dead" were not so neatly separated. We moderns experience the world as so much dead matter, as material for our use. We have, in the words of another writer, "mechanized the world picture" (Dijksterjuis, 1961).

To experience the world as a series of mechanisms presupposes the erection of a certain distance from it and requires, among other things, that we understand ourselves, our very sense of self, as something over and against our environing world. This latter we begin to call "nature": the vast network of atoms and organisms, relays and pulleys, that functions beneath our scientizing—or, more accurately, technologizing—gaze. The world becomes a big machine, and we are its ghosts. But this is just a prelude: For Heidegger, the culmination of the whole process is when we begin, with certain Enlightenment thinkers, to understand human beings themselves to be part of this big machine "nature." Human bodies, minds, and what passed before as "souls" are studied, predicted, and, above all, used as functional grist for mills of all shapes and sizes, some darkly satanic and some brightly painted and fun. Not only the world but now we ourselves are resources—human capital—to be deployed in whatever way. We began by seeing the world as a collection of things, then placed ourselves among them as a natural part of that order. Now we are just one sort of thing among others, a thing that may be useful—or not. (see Heidegger 1977a, 1977b). In this "or not" lie our deepest postmodern nightmares.[8]

We have thus come to understand death not, curiously, from *our own* point of view, but from the point of view of a thing, a material object. People die just like things come and go. Here today, gone tomorrow; I am here today, I will be gone (some) tomorrow. This is a "fact" that I know, just as I know that dropping my keys will cause them to hit the ground or that water freezes at 32 degrees. Notice, however, how the mechanization is woefully incomplete—and radically so. It shows up at certain times and in certain places. Consider the following illustration, a not-so-uncommon case. A surgeon once explained to me that dealing with death, so he had thought, was definitely no stranger to him. He saw people die often, and sometimes die horrible and agonizing deaths in the emergency room, hospital bed, or wherever else he as a physician on-call might happen to encounter them. And as with any veteran surgeon, he had even had patients die as he was working on them, touching them, intimately "close" to them, to their vital organs, to their breathing, to their heart. In addition, he knew very well the mortality statistics for various diseases and their complications. Some were nearly 100%. He "knew" what that meant.

But one fine day during a routine checkup, he was discovered to have cancer, one with a very poor prognosis (as he "knew"). He was terrified, dazed, and disoriented. This surgeon, so close to death on a daily basis, so intimate with it in that way, such a witness to it, had to confront and try to come to grips with *his own* death. Not surprisingly, none of his factual knowledge, his "experience," was of any help in this effort. Knowing "the facts" could just as easily terrify further as give any comfort. Coming to grips is something very different from grasping facts.[9]

We all know that we die. We read obituaries, attend funerals, study mortality rates and life-expectancy data—and argue about the physical possibility of dying with our younger sisters. But it is a very different matter truly to confront one's own mortality; there is a yawning gap between agreeing to the proposition "I will die one day" and really understanding it existentially, actually living Heidegger's ontological difference. One can understand finitude either as a mere fact or as something closer to home.

From this point of view my sister and I were, I think, *both* wrong somehow. I was like the surgeon who confidently knew "the facts," whereas she wanted to hide from the hard truth. Yet in the end, albeit in a privative sense, she was closer to "grasping" in the above sense than I was. Her turning away from "the facts" at least implied that there exists something from which to turn away, something worth fleeing, something unthinkable.

EDUCATION AND FINITUDE

My purpose in this book is to reinscribe into the way we think about education that "unthinkable." I do not mean this in the sense of curriculum reform: adding courses or units on "death education," thanatology, or any other strategy however refined for getting students to think *about* death (although this may be a good thing to do for separate reasons, e.g., Silin, 1995). My approach here is more Heideggerian, as I will explain.

Heidegger (1962a) remarks, in typically gnomic fashion, that a human being "is an entity which does not just occur among other entities. Rather, it is ontically distinguished by the fact that in its very Being that Being is an *issue* for it"; and, in a phrase sure to impress at the proverbial cocktail party, a human being is "ontically distinctive in that it *is* ontological" (p. 32). "Ontic" denotes a way of existing as well as a way of thinking about existence very much like the parsing of the world in terms of "things" as outlined above. Further, the term connotes a more distanced understanding of any given entity: what internal qualities it has, how it functions, its structure—in short, what makes it what it is as a thing or an organism that we might observe in some setting or other. "Ontology," however, in Heidegger's special sense, refers to the study of Being "from the inside," as it were. A proper ontology, then, goes further than merely cataloguing things and people and the ways in which they all interact; it does not describe the way the world "really" is in that sense. Rather, it asks what Heidegger feels to be the neglected question: "What does it mean to be?" Putting two and two together, when Heidegger states that we are ontically distinctive in that we are ontological, he means that one of the observable characteristics of human beings—and our most unique feature—is that our very existence is always at issue for us. Not that we are always conscious that it is; this awareness of our own contingency, our own mortality, is not typically explicit. But it is nonetheless there, somewhere, at some level. It is there "not as a given property but as the constant, although generally veiled precariousness which pervades all existence" (Heidegger, 1962b, p. 27).

At our most human we are at our least thinglike. We are concerned, we are anxious, we worry in the most basic way about our own mortality and, correlatively, in Hannah Arendt's (1958) important corrective to Heideggerian cheerlessness, we are also capable of wondering at the miracle of our "natality," the contingent yet indisputable reality of our being here at all (pp. 7–9, 177–178). Consequently, in all areas of human endeavor, as we teach and learn we build upon a foundation that is itself comprised of the deep and enduring relationship each of us has established with our own mortality. This relationship is usually negotiated behind closed psychic doors, away from the scrutiny of our conscious selves.

I would argue further that education in all its varieties presents an especially compelling case in point. In a book on Kant, Heidegger points out that Kant, in the *Critique of Pure Reason*, isolates the three most enduring philosophical questions, which for both thinkers represents the zenith of human questioning:

1. What can I know?
2. What ought I to do?
3. What may I hope? (quoted in Heidegger, 1962a, pp. 210–215)

These questions, I would add, are also the most basic questions an educator can ask—epistemological, moral, and spiritual; and teaching and learning are in an essential way bound up with the answers. (That is: What should I teach? How should I teach it? Why teach at all?) To these questions, Kant later added a fourth: "What is man?" Heidegger (1962b) writes: "But Kant did not simply add this fourth question to the other three, for he says: 'Basically, all these can be classified under anthropology, since the first three are related to the last'" (pp. 214-215). The reason for this is that the first three presuppose something into which only the last inquires directly, namely, the inherent *finitude* of human existence. What is the teacher? The learner? This mortal one?

The concern with finitude thus underlies all of education and all its pedagogies. In considering Kant's first question, were human beings omniscient, there would obviously be no need to puzzle over what to learn and what to teach, let alone how to do those things. All would already be known; the activity would be rendered superfluous. If, as the French say, every parting is like a small death, then the educative process is comprised essentially of many little deaths and rebirths: Old preconceptions are revised or thrown out, childhood worlds are surmounted, old perceptions dissolve, and so on *ad infinitum* (see Mogilka, 1994). Neither would a wholly self-sufficient being be troubled with Kant's second question. Moral perplexity is for finite creatures; it is a state of affairs that presupposes a separation between the one perplexed and what he or she ought to do; "a being fundamentally concerned with his duty understands himself as not-yet-having-fulfilled, so that he is driven to ask himself what he should do" (Heidegger, 1962b, p. 223). A being whose "not-yet," whose future, is undetermined is a finite being. As for the third question, hope is something that may be granted or denied to one who asks. Hence it can be expected or not. But expectation reveals, again, a privation of some kind and thus also expresses finitude; a being who had everything—including self-knowledge—would have nothing to expect. Each question is, at bottom, concerned with finitude. The ur-question "What is man?" merely summarizes the mortal kinship the questions all share.

This most basic question is open to everyone by virtue of their being human: "What is a human being?" The most solid and indubitable response is that a human being is finite; we are mortal. If you are human, you are finite. You are mortal. And you are concerned with your mortality whether you acknowledge it or not. This is thus not some transcendent ideal up in the sky or open only to a few, but a form of self-understanding in which all of us by nature ontological creatures are always already engaged. It is just that some are more engaged than others. Some are more aware of their engagement.

If the all-too-human enterprise of education presupposes a concern with finitude, then this concern ought to show itself, however opaquely, through that dusty windowpane that is the messiness and everydayness of teachers and students, school boards and classrooms; it should show up wherever education in the broad sense is conducted, in school or out. The success of my presentation rests upon this claim. In the first chapter I sketched two of the most important ways in which this concern with mortality works itself out through teaching and learning. First was the Platonic attempt to become a "lover of learning" and thereby partake of a kind of immortality-by-association with timeless Forms or Ideas. Second was the sophistic ideal of living on through one's students, focusing on the Other and caring for his or her needs and life projects. In each case, finite human beings—learners and their teachers—bond together to become something more than finite: a united front against mortality. In this and the next chapter, I aim to deepen this analysis and try to view things in a more Heideggerian fashion, more from that elusive "inside." What would it be like to confront mortality, and hence the possibility of immortality, more forthrightly? Or, to put it better perhaps, with a more heightened sensitivity? What might it mean to do this as an educator? I return, then, to the furrows set in the previous chapter in hopes of deepening them still further.

EDUCATION AS IMMORTALITY ONCE AGAIN, FORTISSIMO

The way to an immortality worth having for a teacher, it seems to me, involves an extremely delicate set of negotiations. For one thing, one cannot pursue teacherly immortality too intentionally: It appears so selfishly unbecoming to erect "living on" as a conscious goal. Such a project seems immediately to place me in a crassly instrumental relationship with my students. "Come, let me use you. Be the canvas on which I can paint-splash my immortal self all over time and space. As I inject myself into you, I live on; in you I find a host." I seem to say these things as if I am at it only for my imagined sempiternal payoff. But this is just madness, of course; something more befitting the mad scientist of some science fiction B-movie. At a glance, it certainly seems either amoral or immoral as a guide for how educators ought to conceive of their charges, who are, after all, always human beings and as such to some ineliminable extent ends-in-themselves. No student should be fully assimilable into anyone else's project. Certainly not their teacher's. Human beings have lives of their own. Part of teaching is seeing to that.

Not that such an attitude of morbid self-absorption toward one's life's work is unimaginable, and neither is it morally suspect in all cases. It is not at all uncommon among contemporary artists, who so often feel the need (not always unwarranted) to see themselves as lonely geniuses over and against an undifferentiated, unsympathetic, and ignorant public.[10] Maybe the artist should be vouchsafed his or her individuality, even unto the grave. Hungarian poet Evá Tóth (1995) writes in her memorable "Van Gogh Gives Evidence":

Now I know
my utmost masterpiece is my death in progress
that's what I must perfect
These canvases daubed with my blood
with which I could have starved to death yesterday and which tomorrow
instead of kittens playing with a ball of yarn will decorate
the homes of millionaires
they are merely
the by-products of suffering (p. 36)

Van Gogh's paintings are here merely "by-products of suffering," molted shells of something that once was living, by-products from which it is possible for the artist to achieve a certain pathetic (in the literal sense of *pathos*) and perhaps emotionally necessary distance. But whatever initial kinship the teacher may feel with the Van Goghs of the world (being misunderstood, unrequited by the larger society, losing control over the means and products of one's labors), the teacher and the artist must part moral company before long.

Owing to a tacit and often painfully private utilitarian calculus, a teacher may need psychologically to distance him- or herself from a given pupil—to cut one's losses, as it were—and make the hard decision to concentrate on some students and not on others. Every teacher knows the force of this inescapable devil's bargain. Yet what the teacher may never do is view the student-Other as a by-product, an almost incidental effusion from his or her own project of self-creation. For reasons I hope to be making clear, such a teacher in some basic sense ceases to teach; the erstwhile teacher now proselytizes, indoctrinates, prepares human capital—serviceable by-products for him- or herself or someone else. Tóth's Van Gogh's "utmost masterpiece'' may well be his life itself, and all else but a means or a symptom. But the teacher holds in check such narcissism, however refined; teaching may at times be artful, but a teacher is not an artist, at least not one à la Tóth's Van Gogh. The impulse to overaestheticize the practice should not be indulged.

But what is the source of the needed restraint? As I argued previously, one of the earliest strategies for deterring teacherly vanity—teaching as mine and no one else's self-creation project—is presented by Socrates-cum-Plato. Here, Plato's dying Socrates articulates an allegiance to that which stands shimmering and apart, to a Truth that humbles the (in)famous Sophistic-Protagorean slogan, "Of all things, the measure is man" (Freeman, 1948, p. 125). Yet even this strategy backfires as it collapses once again into self-concern (as I shall show in much further detail in the next section). The vain distractions and *amour-propre* induced by the Other-as-society, even the love of the intimate Other, are obstacles and, at best, only kindling for fueling the fire of a very different kind of love: an intellectual consummation with the imperishable. As Gregory Vlastos (1981) writes of Diotima's famous *Symposium* speech and other passages in the Platonic corpus (such as *Phaedrus* 250E1ff.):

> As a theory of the love of persons, this is its crux: What we are to love in persons is the "image" of the Idea in them. We are to love the persons so far, and only insofar, as they are good and beautiful. Now since all too few human beings are masterworks of excellence, and not even the best of those we have a chance to love are wholly free of streaks of the ugly, the mean, the commonplace, the ridiculous, if our love for them is to be only for their virtue and beauty, the individual, in the uniqueness and integrity of his or her individuality, will never be the object of our love. (p. 31)

Personal affection is something to overcome; the actual, concrete Other must be left behind, and urgently so. For as the yawning abyss of mortality opens up beneath one's feet, as the oh-so-stable earth beneath those feet itself seems to shake and dissolve as death approaches, one frees one's soul (*psuchē*) into the sky—a metaphysical dove safe, finally, to hover and watch the destruction and suffering down below. An unsettling and implausible, yet somehow beautiful dream, this. As beautiful as loneliness can sometimes be.

And quite an innovation, too. Remember: Plato went against the grain of the thinking of his own time and is largely responsible for refining and rationalizing the Orphic and Pythagorean religious myths concerning the soul and its struggle to release itself from the body (see Moore, 1963, pp. 3–15; Caes, 1985, p. 35). Certainly, one would not want to minimize the fact that such doctrines had their adherents during the classical period and many, perhaps, flirted with such ideas.[11] But as alluded to earlier it seems to have been extremely rare among the classical Greeks for this notion of one's "spirit" to be conceived in terms of consciousness, individuality, or anything smacking of *personal* immortality in the later Christian sense. Indeed, there is a good case to be made that Socrates himself balked at such notions (see McPherran, 1994, p. 21).

Thus, despite the literary merits and power of Platonic metaphorics, the detachable and ascending Platonic soul "was never prominent among the Greeks, and was never a serious rival to more traditional beliefs" (Garland, 1985, p. 75).[12] Vermuele (1979) puts it even more forcefully in moral and historical context: "It is part of the Greek legacy to the West, and almost a definition of humanism, that the Greeks found grief, defeat and mortality, when faced with gallantry of mind, to be better than unearthly states of blessed existence" (p. 123). To put it mildly, then, Plato was a bit of a rebel when it came to his beliefs about the indestructibility of the soul; and if he did not invent the notion of personal immortality, he certainly gave the notion a life it had never before had (if the reader will excuse the pun): elaborating the soul's tripartite structure and apparently believing in reincarnation and other postmortem rewards and punishments.[13]

For present purposes, Plato's ideas about personal immortality and the purgative self-practice needed to achieve it are relevant insofar as they may suggest an antidote to the egoism implied by looking to influence others as a means to further one's own immortality agenda. Yet Platonism's ability to function in this way seems limited, for, as I have just indicated, it seems merely to remit that egoism to a different level. But let us give the idea its due; it is, after all, not without its attractions. In Hellenistic times, centuries later, for example, we can glimpse more fully how Plato's "celestial translation" (Garland, 1985, p. 75), or what has been less generously called his own brand of "spiritualized egocentrism" (Vlastos, 1981, p. 30), might operate within a more recognizably educational context. Maybe here, where it is more fully fleshed out as an explicitly educational ideal, will some legatee of the Platonic ideal regain its plausibility as an immortality strategy. Accordingly, it will be useful to move a few centuries past Socrates and Plato in order to examine one likely candidate: the Hellenistic concept of *ataraxia* as developed by the Epicureans, Sceptics, Stoics, and others (see Striker, 1990).[14]

LEARNING THE SCIENCE OF IMMORTALITY:
HELLENISTIC DREAMS

Ataraxia means, generally, "tranquillity" (Irwin, 1989; Striker, 1990), "untroubledness" (Barnes, 1988), or "freedom from disturbance and anxiety" (Nussbaum, 1994). (The contemporary medical term "ataraxia," meaning "symptomatic relief of anxiety and tension associated with psychoneurosis," has its provenance in these ancient sources.) In short, for Hellenistic thinkers, *ataraxia* refers to something like a state of mind, a way to describe the psychology of a certain conception of the good life (*eudaimonia*), the proper goal of human living. This state of mind can only be achieved by purging oneself from the anxieties that permeate human life through and through. For Epicurus (341–271 B.C.), probably the first philosopher to think of the good life in terms of achieving *ataraxia* (Striker, 1990, p. 99), this demands first and foremost an effort to dissipate that most vexing of anxieties, that limit to human logic, reason, and all of life's projects: death. Whether it is acknowledged or not, Epicurus argues, the fear of death impels us in so many ways to make self-defeating choices, thereby diminishing our potential for enjoying what life we have. *Ataraxia* thus presents a sort of paradox for how to conduct one's life: We need a kind of detachment (that is, from anxiety-producing worries concerning our own inevitable death) in order to become fully engaged in the life we are necessarily worried to lose. In this way, the Hellenistic notion of *ataraxia* may be understood as taking the Platonic dream of extrabodily detachment a step further by locating it not as an end in itself, but as a presaging means to a much richer, even cathartic, reattachment that proceeds, as it must, under the very eyes of death itself. Platonic detachment is still a symptom of a certain type of longing for immortality, an anxious longing for an utter transcendence of one's life as one is currently living it, a lifting up or removing of oneself into some beyond, a blessed realm free from want and decay. *Ataraxia* therefore presents a different ideal, which, despite the moment of untethering it involves, is ultimately supposed to be as joyous a *terrestrial* state of mind as it is possible for a mortal to achieve. As Epicurus writes in the *Letter to Menoeceus*: "The correct recognition that death is nothing to us makes the mortality of life more enjoyable, not by adding on an infinite time, but by removing the longing for immortality" (Quoted in Nussbaum, 1994, p. 192). This "correct recognition," it turns out, can be achieved only through a certain kind of education and therefore, as I shall argue, can only proceed through a certain kind of teacher.

To illustrate, I will now turn to a detailed look at Martha Nussbaum's (1994) account in her graceful and profound study in Hellenistic ethics, *The Therapy of Desire*. One of Nussbaum's primary literary devices in this masterful book is to imagine a character, Nikidion, an ancient woman and courtesan, and to follow her as she journeys through an imagined education in the various philosophical schools that comprised Hellenistic thought across six centuries and two societies, Greek and Roman. I will focus here on one course in Nikidion's vast and ambitious curriculum: her lessons on mortality at the hands of the Roman Epicurean Lucretius (c. 100–c. 55 B.C.), known now primarily as the author of his famous poem, *De Rerum Natura* ("On the Nature of the Universe").

Nussbaum begins by framing her discussion in terms similar to those in which I have framed this one: If not Platonic transcendence, what is the correct way to conceive of immortality? Nussbaum's description of Nikidion's soulful perplexity in considering this question is so compelling that it bears quoting in full. It is as superb a piece of writing as one is likely to find in contemporary philosophy:

> But Nikidion might think incorrectly. For she might, as often happens, take a walk at dawn in the early spring. She might feel the knifelike beauty of the morning. See leaves half unrolled, translucent, their sharp green still untouched by life; the sun striking sparkles on the moving surface of a stream. And she would listen, then, in silence to the sweet and deadly music of time.
>
> Images summoned by the smell of new spring air might spin before her then, crowding and overlapping: images of faces loved and mourned, of childhood hope and home, of play and hope and new desire. She would see that morning through all the images, until each tree looked not only like itself but like many things that are gone, and each of her steps was taken in company with the dead. The beauty of things would appear to her under the aspect of mourning, and become, for this reason, the more beautiful and lordly, the more human, the more terrible. She walks, in time, exile from a thousand times, transient on the way to no time at all. No animal could see so beautiful a morning.
>
> If Nikidion saw and felt all this, she might also wish to immobilize the present moment, to fix or devour it—indeed, to hold and seize each thing and activity and beauty that she loves. For it occurs to her that no human being is ever really in possession of any joy at all, not even during a moment. A moment is itself the gathering place for a thousand other moments, not one of which can be inhabited again; it is also composed of projects that point beyond it to moments not known. Even as itself, each time is vanishing as one tries to grasp it. And any one of the projects that inhabit these moments can at any point be cut short,

made vain and pointless, by the world, closing itself against her totally as it has closed already on so much that she has loved and will not do again. Death appears to her as the limiting constraint, the culmination of temporal losses. She sees that she will do the things she loves only a small and finite number of times more. Some she will not finish doing, even once. It is beauty itself, and the sense of joy, that makes these thoughts so terrible to her; and the thought of the end flows terribly back upon the experience of beauty, making it keener and more astonishing.

This condition does not seem acceptable. It is an illness that must, she thinks, have a cure. Perhaps some deeper grasp, some more profound reflection, would protect her. Perhaps indeed there is some way to freeze all of life within life; to immobilize the most important things, and to rise above this condition of abject helplessness before time; to create, within mortal life, some analogue of a god's nonfinite completeness. Above all, not to be at the mercy of the thought of death.

It seems to her that philosophy ought to contain an answer to this problem. (pp. 192–193)

I do not think that what is at stake in the present discussion of types of immortality could be better or more poignantly described. The task of the teacher Lucretius (that is, the speaker of "On the Nature of the Universe") is to show Nikidion how a certain way of reflecting upon death can, instead of increasing anxiety, remove her fear, and with that fear the disquieting sense of transience, of fragility, that appears so doggedly to accompany the all-too-human goods of this world.

The teacher's initial response, however, is like a slap in the face, of the condescending "I once thought that but now I've grown out of it" variety. Even more, to worry over life's brevity is to engage in "self-indulgent, sloppy, self-pitying thought" (ibid., p. 194). But why would the teacher say this? To understand, it helps to take a critical step back, like a physician might do after getting over the initial shock upon seeing a patient with particularly gruesome symptoms: she collects herself, tries to analyze dispassionately this horrible disease, then constructs a diagnosis. This is the proper frame of mind in which to start.

What are the symptoms? In short, they show up as the debilitations engendered by the fear of death, and represent what Heidegger (1962a) and later existentialists call so many ways of "fleeing" from the harsh truth of our own mortality, every human being being "anxious in the very depths of its Being" (p. 234). How might these symptoms be manifest in the being and doings of a teacher? Primary among those Lucretius identifies is an excessive subservience to external authorities, religious and political. Consistent with Aristotle's definition of a slave as someone whose activities are externally directed as opposed to self-chosen, one who refuses to confront one's *self* as a rational deliberator is reduced to a status more akin to that of a thing, a tool, the purpose of his or her activity being determined by someone in charge.[15] That "someone" can take many forms. In a sense the fear of death leads one to annihilate oneself by whatever means happen to be convenient; one escapes oneself by finding meaning, an identity, in, say, religious or patriotic fervor, or perhaps in the more bland but equally effective anonymity of consumerism. Structural conditions may of course reinforce this deindividuation process, from extreme cases, such as teachers in Nazi Germany who went along as they were told with teaching the prescribed eugenics curriculum (see Blackburn, 1985), to those less extreme, such as refusing to question administrative or political (e.g., school board) policies that, were one to think about them *as an educator*, would turn out inimical to one's pedagogical convictions. To go against the flow more often than not requires one to take stock—sometimes painfully—of oneself. "Who do you think you are?" they will ask.

A former student of mine, a principal in a large public high school in an economically troubled community, was handed from her local school board a so-called zero-tolerance disciplinary policy whereby, among other things, students suspended from school were not allowed to make up academic work missed during their exile. Despite the popularity of this policy (among teachers especially), this principal was able to distance herself from the fanfare, the official proclamations to the public about "getting tough," and the psychological pressures to embrace a policy requiring daily enforcement. This principal had the internal fortitude, somehow, not to join the bandwagon so as to maintain a principled distance. One must ask: From where do such inner resources come? Whether they are right or wrong in the end in any given case (a very different question), where do people sometimes find the strength to cut so sharply against the grain? And why is it that so often they do not?

Now it may sound far-fetched to say that this ability to think for oneself—morally, not just intellectually—is traceable to a certain type of relationship with one's own mortality. But is it really? Mortality is the one inescapable fact about each of us, and as such it is bound to appear in any exercise in self-reflection if it is carried through far enough. If you keep asking "why?" you are going to get there. But carrying through far enough may be as rare as real moral integrity; if all roads lead over the cliff of mortality, then erecting roadblocks should hardly be unexpected as an existential defense mechanism—a sound strategy if this is one's view of what death is like. We incessantly wrap ourselves in some apparently larger, less perishable identity (from cultural chauvinism to obsessive rule-following, from living and dying for one's "homeys" in a street gang to political and religious fanaticism). And maybe there are sound reasons for doing so that justify such behavior. Maybe, as the communitarian might argue, it is in an important sense necessary and desirable to join up with something larger and in that way to break out of self-interest and provincialism. But the question still begs for an answer: When we are breaking out and away, what are we breaking away *from*?

Lucretius's answer is, once again, *ourselves*. Consider some further symptoms of self-avoidance: "the fear of death interferes with the enjoyment of such pleasures as mortal life does offer" (Nussbaum, 1994, p. 197). If the worry over life's transcience is unchecked, it can destroy everything. One sees the beginnings of this negating force in Nikidion's plight as quoted above: Life's pleasures great and small seem worthless because in time they will vanish without a trace. Even the mightiest monuments and far-reaching deeds will be worn away in time by wind, rain, and sun—ground into nothing. Lucretius goes so far as to identify typical strategies designed to overcome these fears, such as wealth-getting (poverty seems to mimic the slide into death) and "the blind lust for honors and power" (the heroic type of immortality, one of the most ancient). The drive for fame and money may then lead to all sorts of regrettable sub-fleeings, including "criminal acts, ruptures in families, enviousness of others, betrayals of friendship, betrayals of civic duty" (ibid., p. 198). (On the current scene, one might add the soporific effect of drugs—Lucretius does discuss wine! [1951, p. 110]—and the ever-bored and hence frenetically insatiable "consumer" required by late capitalism.) I trust these forms of escapism are familiar enough. But note how, as it so often does, ordinary language once again betrays itself, as the almost medicalized and thus distanced and safe term *escapism* implies something from which one escapes, a place where, presumably, those of us who are not escaping *are*. Yet just where is this place where we sane ones "with our feet on the ground" are supposed to be? Lucretius's point is that we are all escapists—and perhaps especially those who think they are not—unless we have undergone the proper form of Epicurean therapy. The only real difference among us is the precise shape and form of our escape route. This is because not only do all roads lead to mortality, but the superhighways leading from it are as jammed as they could be—from that unseasonable destination of all life's practices and projects, hopes and dreams.

The Epicurean response to all of this, according to Nussbaum, is to counsel Nikidion to undergo a certain type of what I shall call a "temporal withdrawal" from the world. The argument goes like this: What is most tragic in death is something akin to unfulfilled potential or, maybe more accurately, the unfinished projects the reaper rudely interrupts. "He had so much left to do," as they say. This is why we tend to mourn more ruefully someone cut down in the prime of life rather than the octogenarian who has lived a "full life." Thus what is most tragic about death and most to be feared is the ever-present possibility (even probability, depending upon the scope of our projects) that our life story may be stopped prematurely with all sorts of loose ends left hanging. This latter would consist of our unfinished projects, those parts of us that require temporal extension in order to be completed "in the fullness of time," as the telling eschatological phrase goes. Given this situation, Epicurean therapy counsels a temporal withdrawal that forecloses on projects extending excessively outward in time; one cuts the loose (temporal) ends. If one draws in one's loose ends tightly, one has nothing to fear from death. Nothing would be left to interrupt. No projects, no worries.

Assuredly, one could not be an extremist about such a policy; one would have to fix some judicious minimal threshold for what counts as overextending oneself in this metaphysical sense. Presumably, for example, had I died in a car wreck this morning, it would be decidedly odd to mourn my passing *even partly* because the sandwich I made before leaving will go uneaten (imagine the eulogy: " . . . and his lunch-making that morning went for naught . . . "). Yet it certainly seems appropriate to weep because my daughter will now grow up fatherless. In other words, the Epicurean would have to find a sane middle ground between short-term projects like tying one's shoes and long-term ones like, in an extreme case, providing for future generations (e.g., environmental concerns, long-range financial investments for the benefit of one's grandchildren). The psychological and practical trick behind Epicurean therapy, then, is to find a way to divest oneself of the long-term (hence subject to mortality and hence anxiety-producing) commitments while retaining the short-term ones that can, all by themselves, be quite a lot of fun, or, in any event, necessary for getting from day to day. Each Epicurean will have to decide for him- or herself, according to what he or she can truly handle without running into the above-mentioned fear-of-death-induced anxiety problems. Some may need to be "eat, drink and be merry for tomorrow we die" hedonists in the good old stereotypical sense, while others may be able to stand, say, working for tenure, learning to paint, or maybe even raising children. As Nussbaum (1994) puts it:

> The wise Epicurean will identify herself completely with godlike pleasures that do not derive their completeness from a temporally extended structure, that do not link her thus to a world of transient things and to her own transience. For Epicurus does not endorse the sort of hedonism that approves of all satisfactions, and counts as supremely good the enjoyment of whatever it is that people happen actually to enjoy. (p. 212)

This is none other than the state of *ataraxia*, not understood as one thing, but in an important sense relative to the individual (like any other psychological state from pain to happiness to nostalgia), calibrated according to one's constitutional capacities. In some ways it sounds like something to be found in the self-help—if not New Age—shelf of the local bookstore: If you can only find what you are comfortable with, "you will live," as Epicurus says, "like a god among humans" (Quoted in ibid., p. 215). And the key maneuver is temporal withdrawal, wherein one aims to constrict one's future temporal horizon to a psychologically tolerable width. One evades the ravages of time, then, by refusing to let oneself have anything to be ravaged—a holy no-saying that wants to escape time by refusing to budge from it.

This, indeed, should be sounding familiar again. The ideal here seems to contain a strong Platonic residue (or at least a conceptual affinity, whatever the historical nexus) in that the goal, still, is to escape time somehow. In this sense "we see how deep in the daily practice of Epicureanism was the promise to raise the pupil above her finitude" (ibid., p. 215). Nikidion is thus learning the same lesson she would have at the feet of Plato: how to become immortal.

AWAKENING TO THE VOICE OF THE OTHER

And yet the plot thickens, for Lucretius argues that one of the best ways not to be bothered by the anxieties inherent in temporally extended projects is to occupy oneself in as unbridled a way as one can with something as useless as possible: science, which for him means the relatively idle yet potentially impassioned contemplation of the natural world. Consider the following from Lucretius's "On the Nature of the Universe," in this paean-like passage to his centuries-dead mentor Epicurus:

> . . . the keen force of his mind conquered, and he advanced far beyond the blazing walls of the universe and traversed the immense whole with his mind and soul, whence, a conqueror, he brought back to us the account of what can arise and what cannot, and by what rational principle each thing has its power bounded, and its deep-set boundary stone. Therefore religion is abased and trampled underfoot, and he makes us, with his victory, equal to the heavens. (Quoted in ibid., p. 215)

Sounding more Platonic all the time, Epicurean therapy counsels Nikidion to embark upon an "assault on the secrets of nature, an insertion of the human into the realm of the gods" (ibid., p. 216). She should untangle herself from the vain web of temporally exposed projects and commitments that other human beings have imposed upon her and begin the hard but ultimately much more durable enterprise of linking via intellect her finite self with the infinite structure of nature. In a sense that is supposed to give comfort, knowing it is becoming it; "the grasp of the whole takes the knower permanently and decisively beyond the mortal condition, into the value system, therefore the security of the god" (ibid., pp. 216–217). Words like these could just as easily have come from the dying mouth of Plato's Socrates.

But since this is so, the Lucretian, scientific route to *ataraxia* is now subject—at least from an educational point of view—to criticisms parallel to those raised earlier in relation to Plato and latter-day Platonists. What seemed initially plausible as a framework for thinking about teacherly immortality, given the alleged omnipresence of death anxiety and the finitude implied by the educational enterprise itself, now seems less so. For the temporal withdrawal, the "frozenness" as Nussbaum terms it, required for achieving Epicurean *ataraxia* is, both morally and conceptually, deeply incoherent for an educator, and maybe for anyone.

There are two main reasons why. First, there is likely no more anxiety-producing activity than educating because education essentially involves long-term commitments. As Mary Warnock (1992) has argued, educators must always in some measure justify what they do in relation to some state of affairs temporally outside the site of instruction itself, some future; in this limited sense, education is to a degree inescapably utilitarian. This does not necessarily mean, however, that education need be conceived as mere "preparation," in the sense railed against by Dewey and others.[16] So this is not a *crudely* utilitarian point, it must be emphasized (a view of education that I am at great pains in this book to oppose). I am claiming merely that, whatever one's pedagogical strategy or overall "philosophy of education," the enterprise—even its institutional forms, such as schooling—has to do with the *lives* of those who are educated, often children, and never exclusively with some epiphanous payoff limned only by the moment at which the instruction takes place.

To clarify this point, consider the horrifying example of a child murdered in a Nazi concentration camp during the Holocaust. Such a child may have indeed learned a great deal about human nature in the minutes, hours, or days before being killed—"lessons" may we never allow to be learned again—but to suggest that, say, the SS guards were in any real sense educators of the child is morally repugnant and conceptually incoherent. (Whether the guards intended as much—certainly, they did not—is beside the point, as I shall argue in the next chapter.) To educate is indeed to concern oneself with the whole child, not just in the usual terms of cognitive, affective, social development and so on, but also in terms of that child's unfolding (auto)biographical narrative, his or her future. A survivor would only say something like "my education at the hands of the SS" with dark sarcasm. The locus of pedagogical action can never be temporally frozen in the way the *ataraxia* ideal requires.

To express the point in Deweyan language, can one imagine a case in which a teacher would be justified in promoting short-term growth *at the expense of* long-term growth? Consider a more everyday type of case currently confronting educators all over the United States as the reckless privatization of all public spaces like schools proceeds apace. Ira Emery Rodd (1992) describes two Boulder, Colorado, public high schools in which McDonald's has taken over operating the cafeteria (p. 276). Food service in these schools has now become, predictably, more efficient in the narrow sense as it is so commonly recognized by administrators and politicians. Forget for the moment the nutritional sleight-of-hand perpetrated on students.[17] Forget also the maddening inequities resulting from the fact that the federal government will no longer pick up the tab for low-income students (15% of the student body in the case of one of the schools, Fairview High) owing to the fast-food takeover, prompting McDonald's to respond, "Target those students—along with teen parents and the disabled— to staff the McCafeteria" (ibid.).

Forget these things and focus instead upon the ultimately much more disturbing fact that McDonald's seems to be influencing the school's very curriculum itself: "At Fairview High School, McDonald's supplies not only the food but the curriculum: pupils study McDonald's inventory, payroll and ordering procedures in math; McDonald's menu plans in home economics; and the company's marketing practices in business class" (ibid.). The contrast between short- and long-term agendas is potentially quite stark here. McDonald's is right down the hall, and in addition some percentage of the students are working there during lunchtime. A larger percentage of them, one might safely predict, work part-time at some analogous fast-food or other temporary service job. An important case can therefore be made for important short-term, even immediate, benefits to be gained by studying McDonald's in math class. Even more significant in this respect would be the McSchool's hidden curriculum, containing, one might guess, various consumer habits, "the value of a dollar," mild addiction to saturated fats, an expectation that work means repetitive, stultifying, top-down managed labor, and so on. Is the presence of McDonald's in the school, then, conducive to the education of the children there? Certainly the answer is "yes," in the short-term sense—if only one "learns" to function like the trained animal one needs to be at work. But is this kind of learning conducive to long-term growth or does it stifle it?

An *education-minded* partisan of McLunchrooms (one should allow for such a possibility) may argue that there are long-term benefits of the "learning the value of a dollar" and "seeing the way the system works" variety. (My own teenage fast-food employment taught me one thing only: how awful such jobs were and, consequently, how strenuously they were to be avoided.) Learning the way the "real world" works may, from this point of view, be said to stand pupils in good stead for their (likely) futures; there are well-meaning educators aplenty passionate about so-called school–business "partnerships."

Whatever side one takes, though, if the debate is conducted among well-meaning educators (as opposed to those who are really motivated by profit, or some such external good), it will be settled in the long-term arena. If, in other words, it can be shown that one side is more conducive to long-term growth than the other, then that side wins the argument (remembering that our interlocutors are indeed well-meaning educators who have the whole child's interest at heart in the double meaning outlined above). In the current context, then, the salient point is not whether McDonald's actually does this or not, but rather the terrain upon which such an argument has to be settled: whether or not McDonalds-style pedagogy is educative or not depends upon the long term. And this is precisely the terrain where a practitioner of *ataraxia* will fear to tread: The whole child is in fact too long term and hence off limits to the anxiety fleer; education, even in its broadest sense, is altogether too risky a business.

With Nussbaum, one may even generalize this point further to question how the Epicurean could have anything substantial to do with such temporally extending creatures as children at all. The unearthly type of immortality is rendered less attractive still:

> a world without young people would lack much that we currently value in our own world: new birth, the growth and rearing of children, the special types of love that bind the generations, the freshness of young energy and thought, the stimulus of generational interaction in creative projects of many kinds. The person who chooses the frozen world has opted out of much of life's actual beauty. (Nussbaum, 1994, pp. 224–225)

Whatever sort of life would be left to one frozen in the requisite way, it would not be one open to a true teacher of any kind. In teaching, the learner's future always matters.

The second major problem with the temporal-withdrawal strategy, especially in its more scientific-contemplative version, is that it tends to undermine itself by ignoring the conditions of its own existence; it is destructively parasitic upon that which makes itself possible. Imagine *per impossibile* one who has achieved *ataraxia* via the contemplation-of-nature route: lost in the cosmos, taking comfort in nature's imperishability, and so forth. Such a creature would have, in effect, to kick away the human ladder that enabled her ascent, probably while others—perhaps pupils and would-be pupils—tardily grope their own way upward. "For in growing up to the point of frozenness that she now proposes, she has profited from the old system, from the love and care of parents, the concern of teachers. In opting for a world that no longer contains these structures, she seems to be opting for a world in which she could never have come to be exactly as she is" (ibid., p. 225). The sentiments expressed in the quote from Einstein from the first chapter about longing to "escape from personal life," were it carried to the extreme, would from this point of view be dishonest, inconsistent, and self-destructive.

It is certainly possible to be consistently egoistic, though, looking out for number one no matter what the cost to Others or future

Others. But what one cannot be, to recall Vlastos's phrase, is a spiritualized egoist where the "spiritualization" process (e.g., science little or big) so clearly requires other human beings. Where would Lucretius himself have been if his mentor-across-the-centuries Epicurus has kicked *his* ladder away, if he had not founded a school and written voluminously (and so often with the title "Letter to. . .")? In our time especially, the image of the lone searcher for the Truth in whatever context has decreasing plausibility. We have gotten to the point in physics, for example, that new discoveries require large outlays of public—or somebody's—financial support. The search for Truth in this arena may even be stalled for the time being as a result of difficulties in the relevant agencies obtaining funding for the recent Superconducting Super Collider project.[18] At the very least, as Aristotle recognized, the contemplative life presupposes a certain amount of leisure, perhaps quite a lot of it—a leisure paid for by the laboring others who thereby make that leisure possible.[19] The would-be immortal only on pain of self-contradiction may pretend those others need not exist.

The apotheosis of this form of bad faith and the logical extension of the foregoing ideal is pithily embodied in the following from Nietzsche (1880/1982), for whom teaching is "unworthy of the thinker":

> As few people as possible between the productive spirits and the hungering, receiving spirits! For the intermediaries falsify the nourishment almost automatically when they mediate it: then, as a reward for their mediation, they want too much for themselves, which is thus taken away from the original productive spirits; namely, interest, admiration, time, money, and other things. Hence one should consider the teacher, no less than the shopkeeper, a necessary evil, an evil to be kept as small as possible. (pp. 70–71)

This culmination of the Platonic delusion of self-sufficiency can regard the Other-as-student only as a debilitating parasite. But, as I have argued, if this is the stance "productive spirits" must take toward the Other, so much the worse for productive spirits—at least insofar as they wish to be teachers. The learning Other may at times be distracted, a nuisance, a "behavior problem," immature, irrational and even downright hostile. But teaching dwells here in the muddy bottomlands just as surely as at the icy summit; Nietzschean loneliness is far too easy and, besides, it rests upon a lie. However draining it may become to "stand and deliver" to present, past, and future learners, what the teacher cannot do is ignore them, wish them away, or by any other means freeze them out of her ownmost project. The voice of the Other is present even at the outer reaches of what was supposed to be a progressively self-absorbed (and self-absorbing) Truth seeking.

Thus one glimpses how an Other-regarding aim, however nascent, gets generated out of the longing for immortality, even in its most extreme Platonic–Epicurean–Lucretian forms. This demands a renewed and fuller consideration of the sophistic, Other-directed form of immortality more common to teacher-learners. For what the temporal withdrawal strategy ignores, in short, is the possibility of "historically evolving and human immortality" (Nussbaum, 1994, p. 237), one both more attainable and ultimately more rewarding. Once again, I can do no better than to quote Nussbaum's description of the grand lesson she has Nikidion take from the Epicureans:

> For it tells Nikidion that she should live her life in a spirit of concern for the other members of her kind and for other living beings. Thinking this way, she will be less likely to go toward death in silence; for she will want, before death, to give something of herself to the whole and the future, in whatever way best suits her nature: as a parent, a scientist, a poet, or a just legislator. Her other-regarding and self-regarding motives fit well together. Just as she seeks for herself continuation in history and in nature, so at the same time she will seek to give to history and nature. (ibid.)

This is indeed a wholly different way of grasping hold of one's own mortality, rich with possibilities for the self-understanding of the educator. For this "seeking to give" is an inescapable part of teaching, that most human of activities. Correspondingly, finitude and any attempts to come to grips with it as an educator and as a human being make no sense without the Other. As the French philosopher Emmanuel Levinas (1989) concisely summarizes, "prior to any knowledge about death, mortality lies in the other" (p. 83).

SUMMARY AND EXTENSION

In the first chapter, I introduced the sophistic Other-directed ideal and its care-based legacy. My next chapter aims to examine this ideal further, for, as already noted, it provides the most common pathway along which actual teacher-learners have worked through their own finitude—far more common than the rarefied Platonic ideal and its Hellenistic cousin *ataraxia*. Here there is no problem of solipsism, of how to let the voice of the Other inside; other human beings are always already there, "on the ground floor," so to speak. One of the most influential contemporary articulations of this ideal in education has been the "ethic of care" advanced by Carol Gilligan and Nel Noddings, among others. In my view, care theory gets something very fundamental to any educational endeavor right. It also provides the starting point and central arena for the carrying out of teacherly immortality as I conceive it.

Yet as "right" as it is, the voice of the Other to whom care theory listens is only half of the story. The voice of the Other, even when it is urgent or soothing, can sometimes drown out something else worth listening to. That "something else" is Truth, that same idol so mesmerizing to Plato and, in their own way, to the Epicureans. This is, as I continue to maintain, a through-and-through *human* ideal— nothing metaphysical or transcendent need be implied by it. But it tends to be a jealous ideal nonetheless, as perhaps only a human ideal can really be; it commands its own allegiances and can grind down the best and most caring intentions. It is thus to a fuller treatment and more extended critique of Other-directed immortality and its limits that I now turn.

CHAPTER 3

Living Through Others

I am those that are no more. For no good reason
I am, in the evening sun, those vanished persons.

—Jorge Luis Borges (1974/1995)

TEACHING AND THE TRANSITIVITY OF LIVING ON

Talk of education seems unable to do without an element of what logicians and grammarians call transitivity; *to teach* is properly conceived as a transitive verb, perhaps doubly or triply so. A transitive verb is one in which the action is said to "pass over," to transfer to an object, as in "I love you." In this phrase, I am not just "loving" *per se*, but I am loving *you*. (One might even ask whether it makes sense ever just "to love," that is, without loving anything in particular, the transitivity always being implied.)[1] The verb passes over to "you," its intended object. To say that teaching is inherently transitive, then, is to say that it always has an object or objects. For example, if one teaches, one teaches some-thing to some-one (though not necessarily a determinate something or someone). One cannot teach in a vacuum.

Here I am assuming something akin to what Israel Scheffler (1960) once called the "success" sense of teaching, as opposed to the mere "intentional" sense (pp. 42–43, 68; see also Soltis, 1968, pp. 42–44). The former implies that true teaching necessarily involves some traceable causal relationship with learning—one is *really* teaching if and only if someone is *really* learning as a result. Partisans of the intentional sense, on the other hand, want to leave room for the possibility that one may be doing absolutely everything right as a teacher—one may *really* be teaching—yet through no fault of one's own no learning is taking place (perhaps owing to adverse material circumstances or plain lousy students). After all, intentional-sense partisans might argue, students along with larger structural condi-

tions such as society and the economy should share some of the
burden, too. This makes a lot of sense: There is no one factor that
guarantees good teaching. But even while recognizing this complexity, I would still weigh in with the success sense, though I would
recast its meaning in terms of the transitivity metaphor introduced
above. Thinking of teaching as transitive has the advantage of avoid-
ing the unnecessarily derogative associations of "failing" to teach.
Sometimes, of course, teachers may be blameworthy. But at this level
of abstraction, if there is to be any blame, it is properly left undecided.
Teaching just *is* the movement occasioning the transitivity—whenever and however that movement comes about.

More, teaching must always be seen as a hermeneutical enterprise (this will be fleshed out in much greater detail in the next chapter): For any instance of teaching to mean something, it must effect a
fusion of the understanding-horizons of both teacher and learner.
Education is a sort of meeting ground between the two, where meaning is made. From this perspective, teaching literally *makes no sense*
without the Other who is to be taught. But by the same token, success
will never come in the unidirectional form of implanting in you-the-
student's head a carbon copy of what was in mine-the-teacher's.
You-the-student will make something of your own out of it, in a way
that is to a degree always beyond my control. I can certainly enforce
parameters—I can discipline, punish, test—but the meanings you
make will always in an inescapable sense be your own, just as they
will remain in an equally inescapable sense mine also. Though calculus is not just yours to do with as you please, no one else can learn
calculus for you, just as surely as no one else can die your own death.
So success as a teacher is not about making that carbon copy—the
copy always also has to "make" itself.

But even if what one is doing to (or with) the Other is to a great
extent epistemically up for grabs (as in all forms of communication,
one can never wholly control how one is heard), there is still an
essential Other-directedness to teaching: Even if one may fail at getting someone to learn a particular lesson, one-as-teacher looks toward
that Other, however obliquely might be the look in some cases.
Teaching must in fact succeed, but success need not mean the faithful
execution of teaching-intentions; rather, and I would argue much
more commonly, success simply means the accomplishment of transitivity, the attachment of an activity on-the-way-to-teaching something to some-one. One can, for example, end up teaching something
different from what one had intended, just as one can teach something without intending to do so (e.g., a moral or aesthetic exemplar

like a statesman or an athlete). But just because teaching may be detached from intentionality, it does not follow that it may be detached from Others. Hence my focus on transitivity: that turning toward Others, the movement down a path toward them, or, as Heidegger might put it, a hearing of the Other's "call," presupposes some prior attunement to them. It is this twin movement that counts, the dynamic *entendre*.

Say I watch someone drill a hole in the ground, unbeknownst to the driller. Say, in addition, I learn to drill a hole as a result. Though unconscious of being observed, is the hole-driller not a teacher then? If one grants this as an instance of teaching, wouldn't it refute the idea that one need be oriented toward the Other in order to teach? Can't one teach without trying to? My answer is "yes"—*in a sense*, for it remains the case that the hole-driller is teaching—regardless of her intentions. This is why I employ the grammatical metaphor of transitivity: hole-drilling *becomes* teaching when that hole-drilling "finds" as its object a learner. (In this way, the hole-drilling may be a great many things, perhaps infinitely many: the cause of an irritating traffic jam, a prelude to disaster, an end to a neighboring officeworker's concentration, etc.) What is crucial is what one might call the semantic (and experiential) "spinning out" of the event to a learning-Other, the connection intended or not into an emergent weblike network of cause and effect. Intending to teach—formal instruction—may indeed facilitate this process, but it should not be confused with the process itself (an error to which researchers in education are especially prone).

Granted, the spinning out may come well after the fact. Whether or not our hole-driller becomes a teacher depends on events that may be well beyond her control, even beyond the spatiotemporal boundaries that constitute biological existence. In a related context, Thomas Nagel has argued that sometimes even future events can retroactively confer moral status on past events. We cannot control the "spin" events place on our actions. As a commentator on Nagel notes, the "failure of the American Revolution might have made Washington and Jefferson traitors responsible for unnecessary bloodshed, rather than national heroes, and Gauguin's trip to Tahiti might have been little more than a reckless self-indulgence at the expense of his family, had he not painted his masterpieces there" (Mighton, 1995, p. 108). Thus it might be said that the pedagogical status of an action—or even the very occurrence of that action—can mutate over time and in relation to events external to that action. The hole-drilling can *become* a pedagogical event precisely by virtue of such externalities. Finite creatures like ourselves are at once liberated and condemned by our own existential makeup, imbued as we are with a historicity assuring that the meanings of our deeds are inescapably beyond our control.[2] As Nagel (1979) writes, "A man's life includes much that does not take place within the boundaries of his body and his mind, and what happens to him can include much that does not take place within the boundaries of his life" (p. 6). In this sense, the "my" in "my life" is always to a degree ambiguous. Ditto the "my" in "my teaching" and "my learning."

Teaching, that most ambiguous of commitments, by definition takes us beyond ourselves. From the other side, too, as learners, we are all spinning learning webs—all of us, all of the time. In order to learn to drill the hole, I had to be spinning a web-strand in that direction previous to the encounter; I was "ready to learn," however aware or not I may have been of it. My hole-driller/teacher was there for me to ensnare in my learning web, the *sine qua non* of which is the existence of some hermeneutical sticking point for my errant web-strand. Teacher and learner, by themselves or both of them together, may be unaware that the teaching and learning are taking place, but nonetheless the teaching and learning may proceed. All that is required are the connection points, the living nexus, the transitivity—in short, the web-strands and their "objects." For, like the eponymous hero of *Charlotte's Web* herself, those strands and their infinitely varied messages are what tie us teachers in with the immortals. ("SOME PIG!," wrote the spider in her web, quite intentionally saving Wilbur the pig's life.)

Consider an extended example drawn from my very own mother, for years a teacher of high school and college English, mostly Shakespeare and American literature. This is the story of one instance of transitivity par excellence, a case where the *sub rosa* connection endures for decades and then resurfaces at a surprising moment. In the late 1950s "Mrs. Blacker" taught high school English at Central High in Omaha, Nebraska. Some three decades later, in the late 1980s, she received in the mail not a letter but a cassette tape from one of her former Central High students, now a psychotherapist living in Berkeley, California. What unfolds in this recording is a testimonial that despite its particularities will resonate as warmly familiar to veteran teachers, or at least to the fortunate ones:

Hello, Marcia, this is Elayne Savage. I guess when you knew me in high school in Omaha you would have known me as Elayne Raskin.

I decided to tape this because trying to write a letter and explain what I need to explain became burdensome and a tape seemed a much better way to proceed.

I'm making contact with you to thank you for reaching out to me at a time when most people didn't seem to recognize I was in trouble. I think you did recognize that. I remember once you asked me to stay after class and you tried to talk to me about whether anything was wrong and I frankly wasn't buying any; I was very much covering myself those days with a coat of armor and I was not letting anybody in. But I remember—it's 30 years later—and I remember and the armor is not so tough anymore. It's taken a lot of work to get to that point and somehow I think that recognizing and remembering that you were one of the few people that were able to reach out to me has been really important to me very lately in this process.

It's interesting how this happened. A year ago, I was in a class in my school. [I'm working on a Ph. D. in psychology, with emphasis in family therapy] and in my class on schizophrenia . . . my instructor conducted the class so that during the latter part of the quarter, we have the opportunity, so to speak, to experience what it's like to have a schizophrenic break. We allow ourselves to let go in a fairly safe environment. In order to do this, we choose a name and write a name on a nametag. And without any forethought at all I found myself writing the name "Marcia," and I spelled it M-A-R-C-I-A. I did this with a slight awareness that that's how you spelled your name. And the age I chose to be that day was 15 years old.

I had a very powerful experience in this class, and in the days that followed, as I processed this with my family and with my instructor, I recognized how fragile I must have been at that time in my life when I had been your student. I have no idea if you remember me or the time that you did try to make some contact with me, but there had in fact been a lot going on, probably mostly based on the fact that I had not been encouraged to mourn the deaths of my mother or grandmother after the plane crash, and also that there were some other things in my life that I'm recently recognizing which have to do with some other things in my life that I'm recently recognizing. As [my instructor] and I talked about it, I said, "you know, I'd really like to contact Marcia Blacker and thank her," and my instructor said, "well why don't you . . . why don't you go to the library and track her down . . . ?" So it took me a year, but I did get to the library and

I did track you down. And I do want to thank you. It was real important to me . . . [At this point, obviously choked with emotion, Elayne's voice trails off and she seems to press the "pause" button to collect herself before resuming the tape.]

As I look back, I try to remember who I was then, things that had gone on around me, and I really have blocked a lot out, but I do remember you reaching out. I remember some other things about that class and about you. I remember how much you like Edgar Allen Poe, and I remember that I had written a short story one time for class about some little kid who wanted to be adopted, and you submitted it for a contest with a pseudonym on it since you couldn't submit under the real name of whoever wrote it. The pseudonym was "Anna Franklin." Actually, I've used it: I was taking an assessment class and did a test on myself that I could do objectively and when we discussed it in class I didn't want to use my real name so I used the name Anna Franklin on the test, which was quite interesting! I still have that story someplace. . . .

At any rate, those are some of my memories, even though I don't have a lot of memories about that time of my life. . . . I hope to hear from you soon, Marcia. I'll look forward to it. Goodbye.

My mother did respond in what has since developed into a congenial, though sporadic, correspondence. At first, she had barely remembered Elayne and had only the fuzziest recognition of the (to Elayne) fateful after-class attempt to communicate with her. Elayne had in fact moved away after that year and had finished high school elsewhere. To my mother, it was not really an "important" event. It had not stood out in her memory at all; in retrospect, she was mostly oblivious to what was obviously a monumental occurrence at a crucial time in an adolescent's life. But she was in the "right place at the right time" as a teacher and as a human being, however unaware of it she may have been. From a certain angle, she did not even *do* much of anything: She reached out in some vague way to a 15-year-old who "wasn't buying any." All she did was care.

Yet in that caring she lives in Elayne, somewhere, it seems, deep down in a place that may never have been uncovered (let alone really acknowledged and communicated) had it not been for the special circumstances of an exercise in a doctoral course on schizophrenia. It leads one to wonder, well beyond the present case, how many instances of deep and lasting teacherly influence like this never come to the surface at all. The class reunions, the letters to an aging teacher, the funerals and elegaic remembrances, however numerous and well-conveyed, these must all represent but the tip of an iceberg that is the mass of a well-loved teacher's influences. The bulk of them are probably below the surface, many of them far, far below, perhaps long-forgotten by both influencer and influenced, some of them, maybe even most of them, never having been conscious to one or both parties at all. The example of Elayne and my mother partially illustrates this: Until her psychology exercise, she may not have been consciously aware of my mother's (in her own retrospective interpretation) decisive quasi-intervention. For her part, my mother had not thought about it for 30 years, and only slowly did she come to remember some of it. Thus for most of those decades neither party "knew" of this life-altering event (from Elayne's tape and the tone of it, "life-altering" does not seem too strong a term). Yet there it was nonetheless, enduring in the background, an important moving and shaping force in a human life. It probably never showed up in Elayne's test scores, never exactly figured into a young teacher's merit evaluations, and never was accounted for in preservice teacher texts and even "student teaching." Least of all might it have helped in the then-frantic post-*Sputnik* race with the Soviets, just as now it would be irrelevant to the national crusade for schools to add value to students-as-products and productivity to students-as-workers. Useless and, even worse, invisible, it seems, are these teacherly influences that live on well past the test numbers, the bureaucratic everydayness of much school routine, and the latest from the statisticians.

Yet still, it *was* there, and I can scarcely think of anything more important. Could it be that the moral core of teaching flies far below our most professional and scholarly radar detectors? When my mother remembers, at the end of the day, what made her teaching worthwhile, she remembers events like these—those precious iceberg tips. Won't all of us? What could be more tragic for a teacher than not to? Ask yourself: On your deathbed, will you take solace in having oiled the wheels of commerce or increased the number of right answers in the world? Or will that stillest of satisfactions come from your having touched a human life?

TEACHERLY INFLUENCE AS A MODE OF CARING

The precise nature of this over- and underground current of teacherly influence has, indirectly, been the subject of intense and voluminous debate in theoretical circles for over a decade now.

Emerging out of the developmental psychologist Carol Gilligan's (1982) influential critique of Lawrence Kohlberg's widely accepted stages of moral development, "care theory" holds that the interpersonal connections, the "web of relationships," that underlie teaching and learning are central to how we ought to conceive of the enterprise as a whole, and that they are, in fact, its moral heart. Since having an influence on someone presupposes having at some level a connection with that person, a relationship of varying degrees of intensity and duration, care theory as an account of interpersonal connectedness may supply important clues to the kind of immortality being considered in this chapter. If, as it now seems, "living on" through teaching must have something fundamentally to do with the kinds of relationships one establishes with other people, an investigation of the nature of those relationships seems in order.

To understand care theory, it is first necessary to understand something of its provenance. Kohlberg argues that the development of moral judgment may be schematized according to six progressive stages, from "lower" levels to "higher." (He groups these stages into three levels: preconventional, conventional, and postconventional, or principled.) At the first stage, one's primary reason for following rules is to avoid punishment (Kohlberg uses the Kantian term "heteronomous"); one may "do the right thing," but only out of concern for the sanction (reward or punishment) of some superior authority. At stage two, one may follow rules in the absence of the fear of coercion-backed authority, but only out of a sense that doing so is in one's own immediate interest ("you scratch my back, I'll scratch yours"). At stage three, the right thing to do is defined in terms of what is expected of one, given one's role (e.g., "a good mother," "an obedient son," etc.). Here, one wants to be seen as a good person and actually to be one in one's own eyes (eyes that are now the internalized eyes of others). This is the "good boy" stage. Here, one may also believe in the Golden Rule and its requirement of sympathetic projection—putting oneself in "the other guy's shoes." Paramount are particular interpersonal relationships and their attendant expectations. At stage four, "social system and conscience," one begins to take a wider view of how actions are implicated in a larger social system; one considers how one's actions might affect society, the group, or the institution. One might ask quasi-rhetorical questions such as "what if everybody did it?"

The penultimate stage five is more or less a utilitarian stage, where the good is determined according to the principle of utility, "the greatest good for the greatest number." It is postconventional because thinking in these terms presupposes some vantage point from outside any particular "social attachments and contracts"; the overall welfare of everyone is paramount. This stage may also house concern for nonrelative values or rights such as life and liberty that should be upheld regardless of cultural context. Finally, the highest stage, stage six, requires allegiance to universal ethical principles that are grounded wholly outside of any particular social, cultural, or political arrangements, and from which the latter may be critiqued. One does the right thing because a universal principle entails it; it is simply right—not because it will bring profit (including the high esteem of others), or because society will fall apart if you do not, or even because the action will result in the greatest good for the greatest number of people involved. One acts according to one's own lights: lights illuminated by one's personal commitment to universal moral principles that apply at all times, in all places, and to everyone (e.g., the Kantian formulation of the categorical imperative requiring that persons should never be treated merely as means but always as ends-in-themselves). Here one focuses upon abstractions such as justice, autonomy, dignity, freedom, and the like (Colby & Kohlberg, 1987, pp. 34-35).

Kohlberg arrives at his description of these stages by monitoring responses, mostly among children and adolescents, to descriptions of moral dilemmas. The most famous of these is the so-called Heinz dilemma, where subjects are asked to solve the following problem: The wife of a man named Heinz is dying but could be cured only by taking a drug in possession of the local druggist. But Heinz is broke and the druggist refuses to give the drug to him. What should he do? Should he steal the drug? A stage one or two response might read, "Frienship is based on trust. If you can't trust a person, there's little grounds to deal with him. You should try to be as reliable as possible because people remember you by this. You're more respected if you can be depended upon." A postconventional account: "I think human relationships in general are based on trust, on believing in other individuals. If you have no way of believing in someone else, you can't deal with anyone else and it becomes every man for himself. Everything you do in a day's time is related to somebody else and if you can't deal on a fair basis, you have chaos." Here is a well-articulated stage six response:

> It is wrong legally but right morally. Systems of law are valid only insofar as they reflect the sort of moral law all rational people can accept. One must consider the personal justice involved, which is the root of

the social contract. The ground of creating a society is individual justice, the right of every person to an equal consideration of his claims in every situation, not just those which can be codified in law. Personal justice means, ''Treat each person as an end, not as a means.'' (Kohlberg, 1987, p. 292)

On Kohlberg's scale one progresses when one adopts an increasingly universal perspective, one cleansed of the polluting contingencies of particular attachments and entanglements such as nation, neighborhood, lover, or parent. The justification for one's actions must be roughly Kantian; the rule implied by the action must be universally valid. A stage six response might be distilled into the rule ''life is more valuable than property,'' which one recognizes as unconditionally binding.

But Kohlberg's celebrated hierarchy of moral development, as lucid and as neutral as it may seem, was severely challenged by his associate Carol Gilligan.[3] In one of the most widely cited theoretical books of the 1980s, *In a Different Voice*, Gilligan (1982) identifies what she takes to be a serious bias in Kohlberg's approach. She is disturbed to note how girls and women seemed consistently to score lower on Kohlberg's scale than did boys and men. From the point of view of Kohlberg's scale, in fact, females seemed in all too many cases to be positively dim-witted morally, often appearing uncooperative, even evasive. Often they would even backslide to lower levels. Here is the response of 11-year-old Jake, one Gilligan argues is typical of boys:

> For one thing a human life is worth more than money, and if the druggist only makes $1000, he is going to live, but if Heinz doesn't steal the drug, his wife is going to die. (*Why is life worth more than money?*) Because the druggist can get a thousand dollars later from rich people with cancer, but Heinz can't get his wife again. (*Why not?*) Because people are all different and so you couldn't get Heinz's wife again. (Gilligan, 1982, p. 26)

Jake tends to appeal to logical categories and distinctions (e.g., his implied distinction between life and money); his approach to the dilemma is neatly summarized in his reported attitude to the whole problem, which for him was ''sort of like a math problem with humans'' (ibid.). According to Kohlberg, responses such as these indicate Jake is well on the way to moral maturity: applying logic to the dilemma, conceiving of the particular situation as instantiating a general rule, understanding that figuring out and justifying a course of action require discriminations based on an ever more universal outlook. All told, Jake is making a commendable advance beyond particularism.

But matters seem to stand much differently with Amy, a girl respondent of the same age. When asked if Heinz should steal the drug, Amy seems, as Gilligan puts it, "evasive and unsure": "Well, I don't think so. I think there might be other ways besides stealing it, like if he could borrow the money or make a loan or something, but he really shouldn't steal the drug—but his wife shouldn't die either." She seems not able—or willing—to make that universalizing move, to see it all as Jake's "math probem with people." Amy continues: "If he stole the drug, he might save his wife then, but if he did, he might have to go to jail, and then his wife might get sicker again, and he couldn't get more of the drug, and it might not be good. So, they should really just talk it out and find some other way to make the money" (ibid., p. 28).

But where is one to chart Amy's responses here? "Talk it out"? There seems no place for that kind of answer on Kohlberg's charts; if it is to be placed there, maybe it belongs down in stage three somewhere, where one is preoccupied with roles and being liked by others. What Gilligan argues, however, is that Amy illustrates an entirely different way of constructing the dilemma. Her responses begin to make sense—a great deal in fact—when they are viewed within a different moral paradigm, "a different voice," in which human interrelationships are seen as primary as opposed to abstract considerations of principle (e.g., rights, justice). This is Gilligan's "web of relationships" orientation, which she argues is more typical of women than of men.

From this new perspective, then, basic to the Heinz dilemma is not so much figuring out how to apply a principle such as "life over property," but rather sorting through the network of relationships within which the actors are situated, locating those that seem frayed or severed and then setting about to mend them. Communication, dialogue, "talking it out," is one strategy consistent with this mending operation. This seems to make sense out of Amy's basic moral impulses, like her initial keenness to avoid bad feelings all around. Everyone involved should get together and set about the hard work of (re)establishing the wholesome connectedness that ought to be providing the basis for their dealings with one another. From this perspective, to use a different example, breaking a promise would not be seen as "violating a rule" so much as it would be "letting someone down," or perhaps "letting someone off the hook." Caring involves first of all looking at our relationships with Others. Care theory builds an ethic upon this basic insight and seeks to end the traditional (usually conceived in terms of patriarchy) delegitimizing and deprioritizing of this salutary "different voice."

The care-based approach to ethics has made significant inroads into educational thinking, largely via its most artful proponent, Nel Noddings. As mentioned in Chapter 1, Noddings (1984) argues that the care orientation ought to be the ground for our deepest educational commitments, that we ought first and always to focus our attention on the Other, the student, the "cared-for." In some ways this seems obvious: *Of course* the Other, his or her well-being, maturation, creativity, or growth should always be the educator's utmost concern. Where else is one to focus? But one of Noddings's main contributions and insights is to show how what might well in the abstract seem obvious—like good politicians, most would undoubtedly assent to the platitude that the "child must always come first"— is in fact not so. For one of the most common ways educators forget their inherent connection with the Other is by prioritizing some disembodied subject matter or agenda (note the Platonic residue) over the learner's concrete individuality.

This may happen at different levels (and I may now be taking Noddings's analysis further in places than she herself would): At the level of policy we may feel that the highest mission of our schools is to reproduce culture, to make sure the "great books" are perpetuated, that the Good News of, say, math or engineering is spread as far and as widely as possible (see Noddings, 1992, pp. 28-43). The worry here seems to be mainly over the state of the culture writ large, or maybe some valued segment of it: One is exercised first and foremost over the sorry state of literature, of history, of "our heritage." Such worries, in fact, tend to be generalized ones about "innumeracy" (Paulos, 1989) or, to use E. D. Hirsch's (1987) famous example, now something of an industry unto itself, "cultural literacy." To borrow a distinction from R. S. Peters (1973), these concerns may be either instrumental or non-instrumental: Typical defenders of the latter tend to be of an older guard, "the humanist right," as Lawrence Cremin (1988, p. 192) labels them, such as Mortimer Adler's (1982) "one size fits all" *Paideia Proposal* or, earlier in this century, University of Chicago President Robert Hutchins's classically based liberal arts curriculum (see Arcilla, 1995, pp. 12-17). In both cases, there is a strong imperative for culture to be preserved and/or renewed "for itself." By contrast, bottom-line-minded instrumental valuers of culture see education's ultimate payoff not in and of itself but in its alleged service to ideals such as efficiency of communication and productivity and, hence, ultimately, national economic goals (e.g., Hirsch, 1987, and, more recently, the economist and Clinton administration secretary of labor, Robert Reich, 1991).

On the right, and more radically, this instrumental valuing of culture also commonly takes the form of a would-be theocratic Christian fundamentalism (sometimes exclusionary in a nativist sense, sometimes not) that seeks above all else to perpetuate certain particular cultural understandings. Analogously, on the left, one often finds chauvinistic and singleminded forms of particularism, such as certain understandings of "multiculturalism," that do the same by tending to define the authenticity of the Other by the degree to which he or she is "in touch" with the valued group; education is valued insofar as it can facilitate the connection. From a care perspective that makes paramount the concrete Other above all other considerations, all of the above-mentioned cultural valuers will in their educational proposals tend to lose sight of that concrete Other in favor of their preferred precast mold, whether that be "Western civilization," "Afrocentrism," "onward, Christian soldiers," or "onward, fill-in-the-blank identity agenda." In their clumsy rush to resurrect idols, to compete economically with the Germans and Japanese (successors in this role to the Soviet fright), to enact Scripture, or to be true to ancestral memory, they will tend to trample the never wholly assimilable particular Other, that "small voice crying softly in the corner which I haven't heard over the din of the others" spoken of by my student Cathy in Chapter 1. From the point of view of care theory, the concrete Other may never be reduced wholly to a "case" to be considered—"one of those."

Noddings would have us listen to this small voice over and against the din, and in her recent work she proposes strategies for doing so, ranging from the adoption of Howard Gardner's (1983, 1993) "multiple intelligences" (so as to respect individual students' talents and interests), smaller schools, and a more dialogical form of teaching (as opposed to a "jug and mug—I the teacher am the full jug which is to fill the waiting empty student mugs—transmission of information, what Freire [1970] calls the "banking model") to the more controversial reforms such as the deprofessionalization of teaching (the connotations of the expert role are too amoral; if we mimic law or medicine, we "will have sold our educational souls for a portion of professional porridge" [Noddings, 1992, p. 178]) and a curriculum differentiated enough to allow those with "academic talent" (i.e., the college-bound) to pursue their path and those with nonacademic talents to pursue theirs. Whatever her particular proposals, though, the bottom line for Noddings is that a major reversal of educational priorities is in order, a veritable paradigm shift: The main purpose of school is neither cognitive nor economic but moral. That means we should aim to develop a certain type of person—a caring one—according to a certain ethical ideal, an ethic of care, of connectedness, and so on. All other ideals—some of them admittedly important ones—should be subservient to this all-embracing aim. Noddings appeals to the analogy of a parent who feeds a child and also dresses her attractively: Both are desirable but one obviously has priority. For her, "the intellect," "the subject matter," perhaps in some sense even "the culture," all play the role of the attractive outfit to the more necessary and nutritive moral ideal.

It is, then, in the truest spirit of sophistic pedagogy (and its critique of Plato) that she writes: "When we deliberately pose tasks or suggest means that may promote the intellect but put the ethical ideal at risk, we have confused our priorities dangerously" (Noddings, 1984, p. 173). The ultimate payoff of education lies in the human interconnections it mends, nurtures, and gives birth to; its enduring value consists in its ability to "live in" those particular Others who are so connected, to make the extension any genuine ethics requires: beyond our narrower and more immediate projects and toward the Other.

To draw upon my parents yet again, let me illustrate something of the power and endurance of these interconnections toward which care theory helps us turn. This happens to be easy for me to do. I was raised by parents who revered their teachers and always had many stories to tell of them, stories told in a certain tone of voice and in a certain mood: from an exacting grade-school Latin teacher, to a neurosurgery legend, to a university professor with a contagious passion for Shakespeare. But, again, these are just the consciously remembered iceberg tips. Let us, then, take another dip into the cold waters below. Switching directional frames from those who influenced my parents to those they have influenced, let us dive in, back to Omaha Central High, 1959, and another of my mother's long-lost students. She relates to me this story:

> I had a boy in one of my junior English classes by the name of Rob Procacci. He was rather a handsome young man who liked to sit in the front of the class but who appeared indifferent to the work. I asked him about his less-than-enthusiastic attitude one day, and he told me that he was repeating junior English; he was actually a senior but was repeating a couple of classes that he

had failed as a junior. He said that he really saw no purpose in continuing with school and was ready to quit. He was going to get a job anyway, so why bother with school? I do remember having a long talk with him, but what I said escapes me. No doubt the usual. At any rate, he completed my class with a passing grade, and was never a problem. About a dozen or so years ago, I was talking to Jim [your cousin] and he told me that he had met someone through his political work and they had gone out for drinks and dinner with other friends. During the course of the evening they discussed a variety of subjects, one of which was high school. And this new friend talked about having had to repeat his junior English class and how it was the best thing that ever happened to him. When Jim asked him why, he said that the teacher convinced him to stay in school and graduate. You guessed it, of course. The new friend was Rob Procacci and both he and Jim were blown away that I was the teacher!

Of course, were it not for the chance meeting of Rob and my cousin Jim, this story would never have been brought to the attention of my mother (just as in the case of Elayne Savage's exercise in psychotherapy described earlier), yet the influence was of course no less "there" for that reason. It makes one wonder how many "Robs" and "Elaynes" might be out there, somewhere—perhaps so many as to reinforce the aptness of the tip-of-the-iceberg metaphor used above. If we, then, extend care theory temporally to encompass this vast network of influences that, after all, certainly count as strands in a teacher's "web of relationships," we begin to see how "living on through Others" is almost built in to the very idea of care theory as applied to education. The Other, the cared-for, does not just stand immediately before one and then the relationship is "over." The cared-for has a life of his or her own, one that is extended in time and space far beyond the ostensible "site" of the interaction with the one-caring. The Other takes what one gives, just as one has taken the gifts of Others before. One thus lives on necessarily, even if one or both parties are unaware of it.

This temporally ecstatic (i.e., extending of the self through time) character of the interaction is thus inescapable in teaching: living on through Others. And so, therefore, is the symbolic immortality discussed previously. It is always part of what we are doing when we teach and so undergo that peculiar engagement with the Other, when we really do undergo it (an entirely different matter from whether or not we are trying to do it, recognized for it, or even aware of it at all). This is not to say, however, that there are not better or worse ways of securing that immortality (aspects of this will be discussed below). For now the point is that, just like the verb itself, *truly to teach is to allow oneself to become transitive*: to attach, to connect, and then to persevere. And this operation is always temporal; it occurs *in time*, as do all of the affairs of finite creatures such as ourselves. One might even go so far as to say that we are more like conduits of some sort when we teach and learn: moral railway stations receiving influence-arrivals and sending off influence-departures. For the tracks go both ways; "my parents' influences" has a double meaning. Who am I as a teacher, in fact, but a locus of influences in-and-out or, perhaps more subtly, an orientation, an angle of vision upon that human-sinewed web that is at once me and more than me?

Memory shows us this and drives it home, as it works to reverse the temporal ecstasis. For there are also the letters coming back. Here is another sort of letter my mother once got, one from one of *her* own long-lost teachers:

> Dear Marcia,
> However will it be possible for me to answer your *wonderful* letter to me??? . . . Was it a surprise to hear from you? Yes! Of course, I do remember you—How could I possibly forget? Sometimes, I'll admit, I can't really put a name with a face! But the face I remember—and also the *name*! . . . In answer to your thanks, may I say thanks to you for [being so enthusiastic that you found yourself] running to my class. I was the winner! I am so proud of you for your choosing to teach. . . . Tears came to my eyes as I reread your praises of me! I do hope I am deserving—Ruth.

To be "deserving." Is this not the deepest hope and dream of teaching, the dream from which one should never awaken, in this case realized in the Other's enacted gratitude? Not exactly to be thanked, but to be *worthy* of thanks. This is the "payoff," is it not? This is what a teacher takes to his or her grave. When the enterprise's temporal dimension is given its due, surely Gilligan, Noddings, and crew have gotten something essentially right about teaching, something that sustains it at its living core.

CARING AND THE TRUTH OF TEACHING

But is it enough for teacherly immortality to care about those Others one encounters as learners? To pose the question in terms used earlier, is the sophist-inspired earthward gaze toward flesh-and-blood human beings adequate to sustain the enterprise of education-cum-immortality? After all, the previous chapter has demonstrated the inadequacy of trying to go it alone: the Epicurean–Lucretian strategy of (dis)interested contemplation. It seems as if the vain Plato-inspired attempt to leave others behind is doomed to lonely failure. A necessary care-ful reckoning with Others, a hearing of their call, forecloses this option. Or so it seems.

I will argue that, despite its indispensable contribution, the song that must be sung here is more complex and polyphonic than care theory even at its best can acknowledge. For just as the Platonic ideal of escaping from earthbound Others demonstrably defeats itself by violating its own conditions of existence, the ideal of connectivity-with-Others animating care theory shows itself to be—and I do not think this is too strong a way to put it—morally and intellectually hollow at its core. Taken to its extreme, I shall argue, care theory is literally contentless. At one level, if it is to remain coherent, it must embrace substantive ideals (e.g., justice) that it elsewhere claims to eschew; compelling moral considerations must move it beyond the web of relationships and into an ideal realm more akin to Plato's. This is where it may be said that a third term beyond the teacher-student dyad arises, one that must always accompany any authentic (that is to say, immortalizing) pedagogical interaction. To draw again upon Homer, that third term is what Athene, the goddess of wisdom, personifies, what the archetype Mentor properly "vanishes" into. Care theory must allow for the arising of this third term, which gives coherence and thus—literally—makes sense of the hermeneutical whole that education works within.

It is here that those most unlikely educational bed partners, self-lessness and immortality, are at last conjoined. (The mechanism of this consummation will be the subject of the next chapter.) Thus, if properly contextualized, care theory's very contentlessness turns out to be a great advantage, as is recognized by Heidegger, still care's most powerful philosophical exponent.[4] For Heidegger, the special place and power of care is intimately bound up precisely with its contentlessness, as our deepest connectivity to others is manifest in a nondeterminate "call of conscience." In Michel Haar's (1993) words, the "call of conscience . . . lets only one voice be heard, which says nothing, communicates no message, and casts *Dasein* [Heidegger's term for (the) human being] back upon the singular nakedness of its existence" (pp. xxvii–xxviii). As Heidegger (1962a) himself writes, *"Care itself, in its very essence, is permeated with nullity through and through"* (p. 331, emphasis in original). In other words, care cannot tell us anything in particular: It can only tell us to care; only under penalty of violating its own presuppositions may care theory tell us for whom we ought to care, toward what our caring ought to be directed, and why we ought to care at all. It can tell us to maintain relationships, but little or nothing about those relationships themselves. In the end, care theory turns out to be much more exhortatory than prescriptive in any determinate manner.

Care theory's indeterminacy is further magnified by a number of largely covert theoretical dependencies. First, and of particular interest in the present study, care theorists tend to underappreciate the extent to which care itself is ontologically dependent upon temporality. Admittedly, Noddings, for one, recognizes the importance of durability—the follow-up—in our commitments to Others. But there is far more to it than that: If we human beings did not experience time in the way we do, caring for others would be impossible. This is one of the central Heideggerian insights: "Time originally is as the temporalizing of temporality which, as such, makes possible the constitution of the structure of Care" (quoted in Haar, 1993, p. 31). Caring must always be caring-in-time (note the double meaning), and thus it is only possible for finite creatures, for creatures who suffer and die such as we; we are creatures who can care because we are creatures who are mortal. Take the maternal archetype of all caring relations: Were we not temporal through and through, what sense might we make of giving birth in the first place, what would be its moral status? Were there no threat to a child from hunger, cold, and other mortal harms, how eviscerated mothering would be! The whole idea of giving, guarding, and growing a life would be emptied of meaning. Care theory must come to grips with temporality. This problem is especially acute in education, where attempting to come to such grips places one squarely into the problematic of this book: the senses in which teaching carries me—as well as Others—through time.

It is, however, the next round of unacknowledged dependencies that gives rise to care theory's most serious philosophical difficulties. As in Gilligan's formulation, care theory's unique contribution to moral theory consists in its focus upon webs of relationships rather than abstract procedures, principles, or ideals. But welcome as such a focus may often be, it skates much too lightly over one of moral theory's most vexing problems: How do we determine the proper arena within which moral considerations figure in the first place? To put it more bluntly, how do we know who or what *counts*? Very often moral controversies swirl around this very question, for example, abortion, where whether or not the fetus is a person is arguably—and intractably it seems—the main issue (Blum, 1994, p. 248). Any moral theory worth its salt must attempt to draw the charmed circle properly. Symptomatically, care theorists such as Noddings have great difficulty in this area, drawing the circle too narrowly (early Noddings, 1984; see Tronto, 1995, pp. 110–111) or even denying the need to draw a circle at all (later Noddings, 1992, passim), perhaps being loathe to play that "masculinist" game of separating insiders from outsiders.

Try as one might, though, the need to make such distinctions will not go away. For it is obviously possible to err here. Gilligan, for example, suggests that what really counts are our particular commitments to concrete individuals. Presumably this means those with whom we have some more or less direct interaction. So who exactly constitutes my web of relationships? If I am a suburbanite, are distant others in the downtown ghetto less worthy of my moral efforts because they are not and perhaps will never be "particular Others" to me? Does my obligation always decrease in proportion with my lack of contact with the Other? My web of relationships, in short, may exclude the most needy because they happen to be outside of any real relation to me. Why care about the homeless in Manhattan if I never go into the city? Why care about ghetto schools if those in my suburb are doing just fine? The most likely response, of course, is that we should in fact be caring about these people, too. And that most certainly sounds compelling. But to the care theorist it must be asked, *why* then? The best rejoinder, in all probability, would be something like, "we are related to them because they are human beings, too." This, however, is supposed to be out-of-bounds for the principles-eschewing care theorist, for it is to invoke a patently nonparticularistic ideal, even a covert metaphysics, concerning who is or is not a person. As Will Kymlicka (1990) writes, one would then be attending to particularity, "but only on the basis of a universal conception of humanity" (p. 271). To avoid excessive provincialism, then, care needs to incorporate some abstract category, "the human being"—just the sort of enterprise it claims with such gusto to avoid.[5]

Thus it is not surprising to find Noddings falling back into the other extreme, by prescribing that we care about not only every-one, but every-thing, too: ideas, animals, plants, the earth, even machines. To be sure, Noddings (1992) realizes that caring, say, for machines "is not the same as caring for human beings" (p. 139). But nonetheless we should be caring in some form about everything in our environment, whether it be animal, vegetable or mineral (or immaterial altogether, for that matter). What sense does this really make, though? For starters, one wonders if a theory that tells us simply to care about everything really is telling us anything at all. What has changed for me now that I know I ought to care for everything? More importantly, this limitless inclusivity robs me of the ability to make the distinctions necessary for any intelligently conceived moral action. This is perhaps easiest to see in care theory's inability to handle moral conflicts involving independently justifiable allegiances.

Take a classic case from Sophocles's *Antigone*: the protagonist Antigone's defiance of King Creon's decree against burying the traitor and rebel Polynices, who happens also to be her brother. Not that Antigone herself does (she is a bit of a fanatic), but most of us would see this as a dilemma of major proportions: On the one hand, there are religious and familial obligations that must be honored, and on the other hand, the obligations arising from the political community. Both of these express relations aplenty, but the expectations surrounding each involve different sets of "constituents." Whatever the outcome, most major moral theories would give one something to go on in "right versus right" situations like this. A utilitarian will calculate the welfare surrounding the act or the rule the act instantiates, a Kantian will apply as judiciously as possible certain moral ground rules, a virtue theorist may need to ascertain "who she really is" (pious sister or loyal citizen?) to make the choice, and so on. But care theory seems unable even to begin to help, for it is hard-pressed to make any qualitative distinctions between or among relationships of various kinds. I care about my family and I care about my neighbors, and that is that. No more can be said. To say which groups should count more involves making the kinds of distinctions unavailable to the care theorist. If I am not rendered morally catatonic, then, I am left to act purely out of impulse, with no hope of being able to justify what I have done.

For present purposes, it will suffice to mention two further sets of unfortunate consequences stemming from care theory's rejection of principles-based moral thinking, its claim to get along without abstract ideals (see, e.g., Noddings, 1984, pp. 100–101). One of these is of general concern, while the other is of special concern to educators. First, without recourse to some principle or ideal of justice, it is difficult to see how care theory can distinguish, as it ought, between what Kymlicka (1990) calls "subjective hurt" and "objective unfairness" (pp. 276-284). Care theorists usually argue that women—for whatever historical, developmental or, perhaps, genetic reasons— tend to be motivated more by the former than the latter. Consequently, the various ethics of care tend to regard subjective hurt as a sounder basis than justice for moral claims.[6] But subjective hurt is not so innocent; it can very easily hide oppression by obscuring the question of desert. We are all moved to tears by Scarlett O'Hara's downfall in *Gone with the Wind*, but in real life should we extend our compassion equally to, say, the freed slave and the newly dispossessed (and hence "suffering") slaveowner? During the initial stages of our daughter's infancy, it certainly pained me more to change her diapers than it did my wife (no doubt traceable to our gendered cultural conditioning, etc.) but, during one of those 3 A.M. diaper changings, or at any other time, was my greater subjective hurt entitled to one ounce more consideration than my wife's? An adequate response, in both cases, seems something like a decidedly dispassionate "get over it." The scales of justice simply do not allow the subjective hurt of oppressors—even erstwhile and penitent ones—equal weight with that of those they have been oppressing. Yet one cannot see this without importing some ideal of justice.

In an educational context, one wonders whether caring, even compassion, might not at times occlude other ideals, ones less tied to particular Others but nonetheless compelling. What about the allegiance one as a teacher might have to the integrity of one's subject matter, to Truth—or at least to Truth-as-I-see-it. For example, may I lie to a student if I think it will help him in some way? Say I teach American history, and in order to reach this student, I give her what Arthur Schlesinger, Jr. (1992) provocatively labels the "there's-always-a-black-man-at-the-bottom-of-it-doing-the-real-work approach to American history" (p. 61). Behind the Boston Massacre, for example, there is Crispus Attucks (actually quite a minor figure), who is made to appear responsible for setting the whole thing off (Lind, 1995).[7] In short, I proceed with it foremost in my teacher's mind that there *must* somewhere be an underrepresented "type" matching my student's, behind every great invention, discovery, deed, and so forth.[8] On a larger and consequently even cruder scale, all that is good about, say, the ancient Greeks (and therefore the West as a whole) just *had* to come from Africa–Egypt. Black Athena or no, it might be said that it would be necessary to invent her, had Martin Bernal (1987) not suggested it in his famous book. Believing in Black Athena—the "Afroasiatic" roots of Western culture—is good for us, and that is that. (To make sure I am expressing this clearly: Bernal's work may be good history or it may not be, but its widespread and often dogmatic acceptance among nonhistorians obviously has more to do with well-intended politics than it does with scholarship. As a sympathetic but cautious classicist is alarmed to note, Bernal's claims "are being adopted enthusiastically and uncritically by many non-classicists precisely because of its ideological congeniality, impressively enhanced by the academic credentials and broad learning of its author" (Levine, 1992, p. 457).)[9] Motivated by the best and most caring of intentions, I will tell apocryphal tales, or maybe make up a few of my own: All because they will help this student by augmenting her self-esteem. She will now "see herself in the curriculum"— whether she is really there or not (or, more precisely, whether he is there in the way he is being told).[10]

Noddings (1984), for one, would seem to have no hesitation regarding a case such as this, given that for her the learner is "always . . . more important, more valuable, than the subject (p. 174)" and "the disciplines themeselves should play a peripheral or instrumental role in the education of most students" (1992, p. 175).[11] Since an instrument that does not work should be abandoned or refashioned to meet the need at hand, it would seem that educators therefore have license to "shape" the subject matter however they may need to. In one way, of course, this seems unobjectionable: If we are within the realm of pedagogy, that is, how best to present that subject matter, it seems reasonable to provide for a large area within which finessing that material (fitting it to one's audience, etc.) is not only permissible but necessary and desirable. But if there is no sense at all in which the subject matter may be said to have been violated (no sense in which it may be true or not), then it is hard to see how any parameters whatsoever could be in place; teachers would have a moral carte blanche to teach whatever pack of lies they desired to, so long as it was "helpful" to the student before them. This is the pedagogy of the noble lie, however much it may adorn itself with the jewelry of the good fight against hegemonic power, domination, and the rest of it.

As against this idea that the teacher has in any sense a stand-alone obligation to tell the truth about what she is teaching, it might be objected that the truth obligation is itself still in the end grounded in the welfare of the learner in question. One is obliged to teach the truth, so the objection runs, because spreading untruths will rebound to the ultimate detriment of the learner; in the long run, the truth will get out, and when it does the consequences will be debilitating, functionally and/or psychologically. It just cannot be that lies could really help anyone. This seems to me, however, to rest upon quite an unjustified—though deeply rooted—faith in some sort of metaphysical conception of justice as the balancing of cosmic scales, "what goes around comes around."[12] For why should we presume it impossible to live a perfectly "healthy" life (one full of self-esteem, success, and a host of other goods) that is based upon a few well-chosen educated lies, noble or not. Many Americans suffer from the idea that they are "rugged individualists" who have gotten to where they are due solely to their individual merit, owing nothing to social privileges associated with being, say, male, white, middle-class, and so forth. Such persons are in an important sense living a lie, but it is hard to see how it is a debilitating one (to them). If anything, it may well grease the wheels of their activity, whereas the truth of social inequality, how the game is rigged from the start, would more likely cause a breakdown in the successful (or functional enough) ideational web they have spun around their own lives. As Nietzsche (and, ironically, Plato, too) notes at length, the truth may be harmful and falsehoods helpful, both in the context of individual lives and whole forms of life. Would that it were true that liars always get caught and cheaters never win!

It might be argued more subtly that a person living a lie is *morally* harmed by the mere fact of living the lie. Say I am heir to the throne of England only because my father, unbeknownst to me (perhaps even before I was born), had arranged for the murder of my cousin, the king's son and would-be heir. It might be that my father got away scot-free and no one ever found out; I live out my life convinced I am the rightful heir. Yet in considering the case from the present position of omniscience, it does seem that something would be amiss here. It may be even clearer imagining cases like this one on a larger scale: Imagine a victorious Nazi Thousand-Year Reich that after the World War was able to expunge for its own people all traces of the Holocaust. This nightmare "what-if" future might include happy German children on a field trip to an anthropological museum exhibiting that once-upon-a-time Jewish culture; maybe those same children would set up sports teams with nicknames drawn from the mythical Twelve Tribes of Israel, and so on. Granted, the issue of historical memory and how individual responsibility may relate to it is complex. But it seems to me that our youthful German field-trip goers—however healthful and happy they are, and whatever bright futures they may have ahead of them—are so deeply intertwined with an intergenerational big lie (not to mention the original horror) that they would be somehow morally impaired. At a certain point, they *are* that lie, and its monumental facticity dwarfs whatever they may achieve on their own, however "good" they may be(come) otherwise. They are "living a lie." Consequently, they themselves have been harmed—even though they themselves have done nothing but been lied to.

Would such a case count against my argument that lies in and of themselves are not harmful? There are two main reasons why this would seem not to be the case. First, I do not mean to argue that lies are *never* harmful, only that they need not be. Surely all of us go around with lots of ill-founded and often outright false but in the end harmless nonsense in our heads. Many of these items were taught to us at one time by someone else. If I carry around with me even one harmless falsehood or, even more, some useful fiction, that would be sufficient to establish the proposition that being taught a lie need not be harmful. Lacking sufficient confidence in the veracity of each and every one of the—who knows?—millions of beliefs I must have, this seems a safe enough bet. Second, and more importantly, in the Nazi children case described above, I would suggest that what informs our intuitive recoil—alongside the enormity of the original evil itself—is a plainer, less encumbered sense that what they think just is not *true*, and apart from whether or not it is good *for them*, it is not good in some larger sense. Take a morally less complicated set of children, one whose individual lives are shaped in no obvious way by their ancestors' crimes. Let us suppose this group of children has been made to believe in purple unicorns that play cards, drink elderberry wine, and any number of more or less elaborate beliefs that might come to surround such a myth. All of this may of course be rather charming, and we may even welcome such flights of fancy, chalking the whole thing up to healthy imaginations and the like. But at some point, perhaps at the right age—and even if the unicorn belief does not infect the childrens' other true beliefs—the teacher in us will not wish the belief to persist indefinitely but will want to call a halt to the charade.

To put a fine point on it, then, I am claiming that this teacher would be misidentifying the intuition in favor of correcting the (harmless) unicorn myth as necessarily being grounded in the welfare of the student. Rather, that intuition ought to be understood as at least in part a sort of "will to truth," as Nietzsche (1887/1974, p. 281) terms it. For a teacher, it is simply good that the students know the truth about unicorns; at some point they should come to understand that unicorns do not exist nor have they ever—even if this causes a tear or two, even if knowing the truth about unicorns does not help them in any subsequent way. Teachers have an interest in the Truth, one not so neatly reducible to the interests of the Other.

EDUCATION, AUTHENTICITY, IMMORTALITY

But how to weave together the Truth and the Other, the one seeming such a bloodless abstraction, the other sunken so deeply in the mire of human relations: theory and practice, the ideal and the real, objective and subjective, knowing and feeling, and so forth? If I am right that education involves at its heart these dual allegiances, and if education is itself to be morally and metaphysically *possible* at all, then there must be some way of synthesizing them into one another, of interweaving the sometimes competing concerns, perhaps out of materials that can give weight and durability to them both. Seeing teaching as an immortality strategy, I argue, provides a compelling way to do just this.

My overall claim is that understanding the activities of individual teachers and learners in their temporal context will place us in a better position to glimpse the inherent richness of education writ both large and small. In order to see this, one of the best angles of vision is supplied by immortality, in this study's dual senses: understanding my pedagogical effects on Others and Others' effects on me, and also becoming aware of how the seeking-imparting of wisdom depends upon factors outside of any ostensibly given teaching–learning situation. To put it another way: As an educator, the Truth and the Other both lay their claims upon me, and one may try to seduce me away from the other. As the care theorists point out, it is possible to get sunken into the True and to grow deaf to the call of the concrete Other. Maybe I value some political doctrine, Western civilization, or "getting it right" so exclusively that I lose that Other, falling away from her in the pursuit of some higher ideal. But then the siren song of the Other draws me in: the Other has immediate needs here and now to which I must attend. What does all this teaching and learning matter if it does not alleviate human suffering or, worse yet, if it exacerbates or causes it somehow?

But just as teachers must help, teachers cannot lie, and only the most unjustifiable theodicy will fail to see the conflicts that can arise. Not only must one "speak truth to power," as our contemporary

Foucauldian parrhesiasts tell us (Flynn, 1988),[13] but one must, plainly and simply, speak truth. But truth can stunt and deform; there are no happy-ending guarantees. Thus claims of the Other and the True must be balanced off of one another. Teaching responsibly involves paying homage to the twin deities the Truth and the Other, those jealous twins who tear at our insides and bisect our educator's conscience.[14]

Yet it is precisely in this conscience or, more properly, in this conscience *as* a tormented one, that a different form of understanding oneself as an educator may take shape. The way out (or *in*, perhaps) is first of all to recognize education's dual aspect as it has been outlined thus far, thereby also recognizing that the educational encounter is importantly shaped by something outside the teacher–learner dyad, something that gives shape to and encompasses any pedagogy. In a way, it might be said that the focus on immortality is useful in that it serves as a heuristic device of a sort; it points us outside our usual selves, focused as we are on what is immediate and ostensibly present. In teaching-as-immortality rings true the truism "the only way out is through." Our humanity lies in the extent to which we can point beyond ourselves, both to others (caring) and to the world (knowing). Maybe this is near what Heidegger (1968) had in mind when he wrote, cryptically as usual, that "To the extent that man is drawing that way, he *points* toward what withdraws. *As* he is pointing that way, man *is* the pointer. Man is not first of all man, and then also occasionally someone who points. No: drawn into what withdraws, drawing toward it and thus pointing into the withdrawal, man first *is* man. His essential nature lies in being such a pointer" (p. 9, emphasis in original). Drawing again upon the transitivity of the metaphor of teaching as pointing-out/to (and so forth), or, as Heidegger would have us think, letting ourselves become what we are—that which points "toward what withdraws"—education is at its most deeply human when it is pointing.

Yet what does it mean to point in this fashion, and moreoever to point toward that which withdraws? Some of the details of Heidegger's larger account may be helpful here. For Heidegger, there are certain gateways through which we must pass if we are to deepen our understanding of ourselves; in a manner of speaking we *are* always pointing, though more or less obliquely. And far from being a mystical phenomenon, the outlines of these ways in which we point are clear enough in everyday phenomena, in certain "moods" that may strike us. First and foremost among these is "anxiety" (*Angst*). Drawing upon Søren Kierkegaard's concept of "dread," Heidegger describes anxiety as the mood most revelatory to us of ourselves. In anxiety the world collapses: one's projects and public commitments seem to lose significance, as though having gone down a sinkhole of meaning. Things begin to look odd, uncanny, not-at-home, and contingent.

The French Heideggerian (and later Marxist) Jean-Paul Sartre, in one of the founding moments of existentialism, captures this mood with unrivaled poignancy. In his novel *Nausea*, Sartre's protagonist Roquentin confronts himself in the mirror, and in doing so is struck by this peculiar vertiginous form of anxiety:

> It is the reflection of my face. Often these lost days I study it. I can understand nothing of this face. The faces of others have some sense, some direction. Not mine. I cannot even decide whether it is handsome or ugly. I think it is ugly because I have been told so. But it doesn't strike me. At heart, I am even shocked that anyone can attribute qualities of this kind to it, as if you called a clod of earth or a block of stone beautiful or ugly. (Sartre, 1938/1964, p. 16)

In a strong sense, in this mood the world with which I have grown comfortable leaves me—a crisis of meaning overtakes me. Who—or what—*am* I? Often anxiety—or something on the way to it—may be catalyzed by some disorienting event or experience: traveling in a strange land where no one speaks one's native tongue, the sudden and unexpected death of a loved one, perhaps a move to a new town, starting a new job, even the completion of a project of some duration (that inexplicable feeling of letdown or momentary longing that sometimes accompanies finishing something: a longstanding home improvement project, a lengthy and engrossing novel, a school degree). These are arguably manifestations of anxiety, announcing themselves as so many cracks of varying widths in the usually seamless carrying on of what Heidegger calls "average everydayness."

Anxiety "takes away from Dasein the possibility of understanding itself, as it falls, in terms of the 'world' and the way things have been publicly interpreted" (Heidegger, 1962a, p. 232). This is neither worry nor fear, both of which have some definite object. Here, though, we do not fear any particular entity. Rather, what we are anxious about is more generalized—our existence itself, "Being-in-the-world as such" (ibid., p. 230). Like other moods, one can often not tell where it comes from and how it takes hold of one. It may not be traceable to any physiological or psychological condition. It may, in fact, be an ontological affair. This is indeed Heidegger's view: This mood has something to do with how we understand what it means to be, how we are seizing hold of our own existence. Yet anxiety is usually repressed via various stratagems and is typically considered less sane than the forgetfulness (of being) that is its opposite. The anxious feeling is usually transitory: We shrug it off and bury ourselves comfortably back into our ordinary affairs. A certain intensity in the awareness of one's own contingency may not be so healthy after all. One needs to be able to shut it off and get on about one's business. But however much we hide it, it is still there. "It is only sleeping. Its breath quivers through Dasein" (Heidegger, 1959, p. 108). It remains present, "not as a given property but as the constant, although generally veiled precariousness which pervades all existence" (Heidegger, 1962b, p. 247).

Anxiety in Heidegger's sense, then, is a phenomenological manifestation of our awareness of our own finitude. It is further manifest in the many ways, individually and communally, we flee from this awareness, as discussed in the previous chapter. But try as we might, our very fleeing announces loudly and clearly how preoccupied we are with our mortality. We want to shut off anxiety because it announces the unbearable truth of our own finitude, that our days are numbered. Anxiety wants us to face the truth. Understandably, we tend to turn away. For Heidegger, though, we ought to see anxiety as something much more like an opportunity than we do; it may be a gateway, as I have suggested. But a gateway to what? The Heideggerian answer is that it is a gateway toward authenticity: Tarrying with anxiety in a certain way precipitates in us a change toward "authentic selfhood," a state of being that is possible for us because we are already disposed toward it and, to use an earlier metaphor, pointing that way—even as we flee from it also. In Heidegger's view, we "always already" are doing both, swinging back and forth like existential pendula.

Heidegger is notoriously evasive as to whether or not it is morally better to be authentic than not to be; he seems usually to suggest that the authenticity–inauthenticity polarity is altogether prior to such normative distinctions. One's "level," if you will, of authenticity is properly considered as merely descriptive; it is just a fact about us and the way we happen to cut through the world. It does seem safe to say, however, that Heidegger means to link authenticity to humanness; that is, to the extent that we are authentic, we are more *human* somehow. The meta-ethical question of why it might be better to be human rather than some other thing is left untouched, perhaps wisely.

But if anxiety is one way of pointing toward authenticity, it is not the only one. So is the "call of conscience," which also beckons us homeward from everydayness toward needful humanity, pulls us out of numb complacency, and so on. Having a conscience, an obvious presupposition of any true moral code, depends upon a certain interiority of the self: the capacity we have carved out of ourselves to be guilty, to have heartstrings that Others might tug. This is why Heidegger (1962a) is taken up by many care theorists: As is the case with anxiety, we are at our most human when we are listening to our conscience, "the voice of the friend whom every Dasein carries with it" (p. 206). The call of conscience, too, leads us toward authentic selfhood and might be understood as the counterpart to anxiety, the flipside of the same human coin. In some ways the two are opposites. Anxiety radically individuates me. No one can die my own death for me; anxiety shows me I am fooling myself if I think I can go it other than alone. No-thing and no-one can save me from dying. But the call of conscience is a countermovement to that, as it takes me outside of myself or, rather, opens me up to the companionship, the co-presence, of the Other. It even seems that the deeper I look "inside" me, all I see are Others, perhaps in the form of all those educating influences I have been discussing.

The movement toward authenticity places one in an odd predicament indeed: To be true to myself, I must at once embrace my individuality so radically that I understand myself to be as bounded as it is possible to be, and that means temporally: *I* will die, *I*-am-dying. As Heidegger puts it, I am "being-unto-death." Yet amidst this amoral sinkhole of mortality and finitude, I am also readied to hear the call of the Other, the basis of the moral, that hearing which itself depends on me being *me* and not someone else. To be responsible for Others is to take responsibility and to grasp it one's self; just as surely as no one can die my death, no one else can stand in for my responsibility. In both cases there is no "trading places." Another French Heideggerian, Jacques Derrida (1995), in his meditation on the Czech Heideggerian Jan Patocka (one cannot escape from the Heideggerians!), effects this same mortal synthesis when he writes, "My irreplaceability is therefore conferred, delivered, 'given,' one can say, by death. It is the same gift, the same source, one could say the same goodness and the same law. It is from the site of death as the place of my irreplaceability, that is, of my singularity, that I feel called to responsibility. In this sense only a mortal can be responsible" (p. 41).[15]

Teaching-and-learning, in my view, represents a unique passageway into this ambivalent realm of ontological-moral authenticity, at the same time frightening and exhilirating, seductive though deeply moral, contingent yet durable.

And there is no better personage through which to examine how all this might work than that avatar of all teaching in the Western world, and the patron saint of this book, Socrates.[16] For the character of Socrates, at least as he is represented in Plato's early dialogues, is as close an exemplar as I can imagine of Heideggerian authenticity in the context of teaching-and-learning. The narrative of that life "Socrates" shows us a way of uniting what I have been arguing are teaching's dual allegiances to Truth and the Other: being true to oneself, shunning lies and seeking wisdom whatever the cost, but also comprehending that the seeking must always be done through and for Others.[17] To put it in more Heideggerian fashion, Socrates is able to enter into the mood of anxiety—and in so doing to stare down his own mortality—by finding a way to keep the Other "in," interweaving conscience and the "me" that as soon as it "comes to life . . . is at once old enough to die" (Heidegger, 1962a, p. 289). Socratic dialectic is not incidental to Socratic thought or, as one might better say, a Socratic form of life. As announced in the first chapter, here truth is only possible through other people. Socrates does not sit alone and write; in fact he does not write at all. (That we have any record at all of his endeavors is a matter of historical luck, quite incidental to Socrates himself.) Socrates understands himself to be on a sort of holy quest to find the Truth by finding someone wiser than he. This is the "mission" given him by the oracle at Delphi. His *daemon* thus does not merely tell him to seek the truth, but to seek the truth *in and through Others*—to gaze skyward always, but gazing thus only through all-too-human eyes. There is no other way. Socrates is always on the way to Truth, but he is always thinking along with Others on that way. He is always, in a word, teaching-and-learning. In Socratic inquiry and teaching (there is properly speaking no difference between the two), we have an instance in which the calls of Truth and the Other are in a kind of harmony—one with enough oscillatory tension to keep things interesting.

As a biographical narrative, and hence one "in time," we might even speak of better or worse music in this regard. Socrates has a score to settle, and because of that he is better able to sound out bad notes from good ones. A feel for this kind of existential music, for what notes and movements might come next, places one in the mode Heidegger (1962a) calls "anticipatory resoluteness," itself a further radicalization (that is to say, temporalization) of the authentic intertwining of Truth and the Other, a "way of reticently projecting one-self upon one's ownmost Being-guilty [i.e., the call of conscience] and exacting anxiety of oneself [i.e., the truth of one's own finitude]" (p. 353). Authenticity is to anticipatory resoluteness as dreaming of music is to playing it in (a) concert: a bringing of it all together at an actual time and place. Again, it is making sure one's music-making is "in time," having its own beat while also beating along with others'.

In anticipatory resoluteness, one recognizes that one is both finite and transcendent. The former is the locus of anxiety, the latter of the call of conscience. I am finite in the obvious sense of mortality, and also in the sense that I am through-and-through historical—there is nothing about me that is antecedentless. Yet I am also capable of agency, of being a first-person, of planning, creating, acting, and in that sense rising above what is merely given, making my own imprint on the world and on others. Indeed, as Richard Rorty (1995) points out, Sartre's appropriation of this Heideggerian idea—the famous quasi-moral distinction Sartre erects, upon the model of authenticity-inauthenticity, between "bad faith" and "good faith"—is a spin upon the old philosophical problem of free will versus determinism:

> Sartre said we are doomed constantly to oscillate between treating our-selves as determined (when we explain our past actions) and treating ourselves as free (when we decide what to do next, and whether we like or dislike our past selves). He warned that we fall into bad faith when we confuse explanation with justification . . . and say that our present selves are not responsible for our past selves, or that our past selves were helpless puppets of external causal powers. But, he added, we fall into equally bad faith (and often into religious or political fanaticism) when, with Kant, we pretend that we are, like God, able to rise above accident and luck, when we think of ourselves as possessed of a biologi-cally and historically inexplicable knowledge of the Right. (p. 214)

It is a delicate moral tightrope walk to own up to our finitude and the extent to which we are conditioned by forces outside our control, while also owning up to our transcendence and our ability to make and do things for ourselves and to be responsible. In a thousand ways, this is therefore the dilemma of teaching, too. For example: How can I teach these children of *this* social class in *these* economic straits? The machismo of the males is so strong that as a woman I'm hopelessly "guilty until proven innocent" in their eyes. There are too many bureaucratic rules and regulations for me to maneuver at all. And so forth. But then again I *can* make a difference—me, person-ally—I can do something special, unique with them; I do not need to be bound by the dead weight of convention and the way things have always been done around here. I can break up expectations, overturn ossified norms, do something truly new and worth doing.

The way into anticipatory resoluteness passes right through this dilemma and embraces its paradoxical nature, almost as in the contemplation of a zen *koan*, in which, as Michael Zimmerman (1990) relates (in a book on Heidegger's moral and political theory), a student in the Rinzai sect of Zen Buddhism is required to"solve" an ostensibly contradictory statement. "The *koan* cannot be solved by merely rational means, however, but requires an existential breakdown of the rational ego's way of framing things—and thus a breakthrough to a less constricted, more expansive way of being in the world. This expansive, open way of being is sometimes described as a "still mind" in the Zen tradition" (pp. 219–220). The *koan* here is the moral one that Heidegger terms "thrown-projection": From one angle, we are firmly ensconced in a situation we have merely inherited and in no way chosen (e.g., where I was born, my congenital heart defect, my being raised by Muslim parents, etc.), in short, the facticity that shapes and molds me. Yet I am also able to project outward from that inheritance and seize upon possibilities that might not have existed had I never been around, a version (hopefully less maudlin) of what the Jimmy Stewart character in *It's a Wonderful Life* realizes in the nick of time. I am in-place yet also irreplaceable—as Derrida has indicated above, the ontological-moral site from which responsibility is made possible.

In the context of teaching-and-learning, though, I would correct Derrida's summation that "only a mortal can be responsible" as only an *immortal* can be. Imagine *per impossibile* that my pedagogical undertakings were purely evanescent, similar to the question raised against the Epicurean immortality strategy that withdraws from temporally extended commitments. What if the sublimeness or "blaze of glory" of the moment were enough? If such were the case, it would be impossible for me to *owe* the learning-Other anything at all; all obligations thither would be canceled as soon as they were incurred in a perpetual Jubilee of debt forgiveness. The moral would be shown the door: What sense would there be in holding *me* responsible, in speaking of the effects of *my* actions? I would be the very picture of irresponsibility in its purest form: no consequences to what I do, not *my* consequences anyway; harm or not, no foul. A fully aestheticized search for a good buzz; no seeking the Truth, no seeking the Other, and *a fortiori* no seeking Truth through Others. In the extreme, one might call this the pedagogy of the Great Show: show them, and more importantly, yourself, a good time. Just make sure it is exciting, beautiful, fun—and at all costs an event unto itself. If a little bit of danger or, say, sadism, adds some spice, so be it. That's show business! No apologies and, above all, no tomorrows (cf. O'Connor, 1996). Like Lucretius, I once again withdraw.

But as a teacher or as anyone else, my immortalizing does not vouchsafe for me this negative freedom, this freedom-*from*, for it makes me—yes, *me*—complicit. It makes me able to err, to lie, to wrong Others in lasting ways. It is real life. It is not necessarily a happy ending or a second chance. Just as easily might the time that is on my side turn against me. My immortality, though, may spur me onward to where I need to be, in that authentic *koan*-riddled space of bittersweet death dreams and (a) time that is never lost. In the space where lives are given. Into a place free from hurry and bustle, where I am not a cog in a machine—an instrument of the "they" who want us to do such and such for so and so. As Heidegger (1962a) puts it, this authentic anticipation of one's "ownmost potentiality-for-Being"—what I am calling immortality—combined with a steadfast resolve "under the eyes of Death," drives out accidental and provisional possibilities, "dispersing all fugitive Self-concealments" (p. 357). Immortals do not let themselves be *used*: by individuals, governments, captains of industry, or "public opinion." Immortals do not waste time, as they take in what is given—what is coming to them—yet they also destroy and keep safe, let be and add on. They swim along the current, but with strokes of their own. The wind is in their sails.

SUMMARY

The next chapter will attempt to fill out these metaphors and say something about the nuts and bolts of the kind of immortality-through-education that I am envisioning here. What I hope to have established thus far is that, regardless of our conscious awareness of it, immortality is something that we "do" as teacher–learners, but we can neither do it alone like the Epicureans nor exclusively through other people, our students, like some care theorists might. A synthesis of Truth and the Other is required if the enterprise is to make sense intellectually and morally. I have suggested that the model of Heideggerian authenticity (with Socrates as exemplar) offers important clues toward how one might pull off such a synthesis, as it unites anxiety and the call of conscience in anticipatory resoluteness or being-unto-death (which I am arguing is synonymous with immortality properly conceived). But the question still remains: What is it I am doing when I am "being" authentic, when I am inquiring after the Truth with Others, when I am truly teaching as an immortal? If it is like having the wind in my sails, what is the wind and what are the sails?

CHAPTER 4

The Mechanics of Immortality

I learned not to fear infinity,
The far field, the windy cliffs of forever,
The dying of time in the white light of tomorrow,
The wheel turning away from itself,
The sprawl of the wave,
The on-coming water.

—Theodore Roethke (1975)

THE RACE AGAINST TIME

It is a truism that in large part one teaches as one has been taught. In my own case, as an undergraduate, my courses were mostly conducted in the standard lecture–discussion format: A professor would lecture, usually from notes, and then leave some time over for questions from the "audience." When I began my graduate studies in philosophy this pattern remained, though the segment given over to questions and answers tended to grow, especially in seminars, where often the lectures were dispensed with entirely. In the best of the seminars, the course content—Hegel's social and political theory, Kant's views on space and time, the notion of authority in contemporary political philosophy, liberalism and education—would work itself out more dialogically, precisely through the students' questions and the professors' answers (or, as was often the case, the professors' further questions). And sure enough, when I began teaching undergraduates myself and then later running seminars of my own, I found myself repeating this pattern. This was, and still is in important respects, my guiding image of what teachers and in particular professors do—the best of them and, alas, the worst of them, too.

In and of itself, this is an unremarkable set of observations. Of infinitely greater interest are the reasons *why* such patterns tend to repeat themselves and, on a larger scale, why there very often exists such a "constancy" in teaching practices, to borrow a term from the educational historian Larry Cuban (1993). Cuban argues the common-sensical but often overlooked point that the choices teachers can and do make take place within social, political, organizational, and economic "situational constraints" that set the parameters within which practice must move. However frustrating to each jawbone-of-an-ass-wielding generation of school critics, there is a sort of practical wisdom to the stability of much teaching, one that may even serve key political purposes, perhaps even as forms of resistance to oppressive external forces (A. Gitlin & Margonis, 1995). What interests me here, however, is not so much the world-intruding pragmatic contexts that may necessitate maintaining certain teaching practices, discarding others, and so on. Rather, I would like to focus more abstractly on the deeper, almost ritual-like elements and rhythms that define any and all educational experience. For it is here where the worlds meet— the worlds of Truth and of the Other—that education's covert immortality agenda becomes manifest.

Baldly stated, the grand thesis of this book is that when one educates or is educated, one does so outside of time; in teaching and learning one is immortal. It is not just that I-the-teacher impart something to you-the-student, and then that, so to speak, "part of me" lives on in you. Portions of the preceding discussion, admittedly, may suggest as much. But this is misleading, for it presupposes too linear an image of temporality: a sort of sub- or superstructure or scaffolding supervening upon events, one consisting of a series of now-points somehow strung together in and through events like beads on a string. Past events are, say, beads to the left, the future events beads to the right. Immortality would be like jerking one point of this time-string and watching the ensuing string-ripple hasten forward to eternity. One wins the immortality game if one's ripple— one's influence, one's effects—races forward and keeps on going, going, and going. Absent some eschatological–Judgment Day finish line, this kind of immortality would essentially be little more than an endurance race. By sticking around long enough, you win.

But this linear picture hardly seems plausible. For one thing, by its own standards it seems hopeless; immortality as temporal permanence provides a Sisyphean ever-receding goalpost. For one can never get there. If time is an infinite series of now-points, how could anyone's influence be said to endure forever?—except perhaps in the trivial physics sense of one being the cause of something, and then that something causing something else, *ad infinitum*—cosmic dominos: the proverbial butterfly flapping its wings in Central Park and, through a long enough chain of events, eventually "causing" a rain-storm in China. Even if one ruled out the trivial physical causal rip-ples shared by plant, animal, and mineral alike, and focused instead upon more substantive intersubjective or cultural influences, in-stances in which one might be said to have, as it were, made one's mark on the world, that mark would still dissolve in time like a tideswept sand castle. No matter how large one's influence, no mat-ter how world-historical one's movements through the world, that world must end at some now-point. Ashes to ashes, dust to dust; Moses, Caesar, and Napoleon just have bigger sand castles.

But they too shall pass. Maybe the earth itself will get hit by an asteroid and extinguish our descendants as unceremoniously as the dinosaurs; maybe the sun when it inevitably expands in its fiery dying phases will incinerate those who made it past the asteroid; maybe some dread disease or nuclear war will finish us off well be-forehand. Averting such disasters, we may well figure out how viably to get off the planet eventually and—who knows?—download our-selves onto some new non-carbon-based material. But these things would only prolong our run at sticking around, exciting and interga-lactically death-defying as that run might be. Eternity is a long time. Humanity will die, and with it yours, mine and all our progeny's best- and worst-laid schemes will, as in the poem, "gang aft a-gley" (Burns, 1785/1969).

But Western conceptions of immortality, from orphism to the New Testament, have traditionally required this linear picture, though a souped-up version of it—usually in the form of some escha-tological end-point. One, or everyone all at once, somehow crosses a metaphysical divide: trumpets blare, horsemen ride, Christ judges, and the rest of it. Typically this means *personal* immortality, too, and one's prospects for it are usually tied to how well one has behaved (save some notable exceptions, outstanding among them being Re-formation-style Calvinism, in which everything is predetermined). Strictly speaking, of course, in most forms of Christianity, immortal-ity *per se* is not the issue; what one needs to worry about is *where* one will be spending eternity. But whatever the theological details, all of this depends upon the final *eschaton*, the end-point, the existence of which itself depends upon time as the above-mentioned string of now-point beads; at some point the beads have to end, and it is God who holds the rope. On this conception, immortality is literally getting to God, "making it" there.

Indeed, as the historian of religion Mircea Eliade (1960) has ar-gued, it is Christianity with its eschatological underpinnings that is largely responsible for the historicized nature in which we in the West conceive of and experience temporality (pp. 153–154). One of the great innovations of the Christian worldview derives from its grand extension of the ancient Jewish notion of a people with its own story (namely, the waxings and wanings of its divine covenant): the understanding of ourselves and our world as *historical*, that is, as having "ages," "epochs," even as developing toward some goal (teleology). In short, thanks to the biblical tradition, we have come to see ourselves as part of something called history, something that is capable of progressing or regressing, pre- and/or post-, something that marches onward, perhaps even upward toward some culminating event (e.g., Second Coming, Apocalypse, Revolution). It is thus not surprising that when most of us think of immortality, we think in these prelaid conceptual ruts: immortality is something like a *personal* achievement, a sort of time-traveler-survivor's merit award, a crossing of that eschatological finish line. Winning at the immortality game is strapping ourselves in for some deity-induced, beatific, hyperspace overdrive that leaves far behind what Eliade calls "the terror of history," with all the latter's mundane comings and goings, decayings and hardships, births and deaths. One ascends, chariots and all, to heaven.

In a faithless age, though, sorting through all this is much trickier. For one thing, there is no one there holding the other end of the temporal bead-string: "Whither is God? . . . I will tell you. *We have killed him—you and I,*" in the words of Nietzsche's madman (Nietzsche, 1887/1974, p. 181). No more beatitude, no more hyperspace, no more heaven. All that seems left of the epochal hope for immortality is the part about lasting a long time, mere endurance. There is no longer a metaphysical finish line to cross, just a race to run—a race that can never end (except perhaps in (im)personal oblivion). Remaining are all the trappings of the eschatological view, but minus the reward and Reward Giver. Yet with the Godhead lopped off, what an empty idea immortality as temporal permanence now seems: As long as there is a part of me darting about through subsequent generations, then I am immortal. But so what? The teaching subcategory of this banality would mean that as long as enough of me is passed on to my students, and then theirs, hopefully *ad infinitum*, I've made it, I've achieved it, I've won. But, again, so what? What a pyrrhic victory if there are no more forevers. Just a sticking around of one's influence. Just being around for a long time. *Staying there.*

But why should anyone should find a prospect like this attractive? On the one hand, it still seems only a postponement of the inevitable; however massive one's influence, humanity's days are in the infinite run numbered. And on the other hand, to raise again O'Connor's (1996) point from the preceding chapter in a more general way: Why should being around for a long time be preferable to being around for a short time, or, indeed, being around for just a damn good moment or two, the proverbial blaze of glory? Sometimes exiting, and exiting completely, is the right thing to do; sticking around too long may even retroactively detract from those all-too-few good moments, like the dinner guest who does not know when to say good-bye, or the joke told too many times to be funny anymore. Why this fixation on durability, on what Joseph Campbell (1988) derisively calls "the everlasting" (as opposed to "the eternal")?

My wife and I call it the "shrimp cocktail syndrome." Both of us cherish shrimp cocktail (the ultimate experience being the "Spicy Shrimp" at Shaw's Crab House in Chicago). Any time we order it, like drug addicts impatiently readying a syringe, we will carefully shell, cut, and apportion our three, four, maybe five precious shrimp apiece. We have come to understand, though, that one immutable law about shrimp cocktail appetizers is that *there is never enough*. And indeed there never is. Once, however, in an unconditional surrender to gluttony, we decided we would buy *several pounds* of shrimp. What could be better? Infinite shrimp! Eternal cocktail sauce! We will never run out! But as one might imagine, being stuffed to the gills with what we always thought we wanted more of was a horrible experience. In the clear-eyed wisdom brought by our subsequent (and previously unimaginable) shrimp cocktail revulsion, we realized that an inseparable part of the joy of shrimp cocktail lies precisely in its finitude. That craving to have more—our care at apportioning fair shares, the deliberateness of every cocktail sauce dip and lemon squeeze, the sorry afterwards nibbling at an empty lettuce bed—is not just a *lack* of shrimp cocktail and nothing more. The craving, the incompleteness, the wanting of more, in an ineliminable sense *is* the shrimp cocktail. Sufferers from the shrimp cocktail syndrome want what they simply cannot have, what it makes no sense even to want: an infinite amount of what is by its nature finite. You can have one but not both.

In relation to teaching, it may well be that the shrimp cocktail syndrome is widespread enough, and I would hate to think that this book on immortality would add fuel to that fire. The novelist Richard Ford describes the problem with his characteristic deadpan eloquence. His protagonist, Frank Bascombe, is reflecting upon a stint teaching literature as a visiting instructor at a small New England liberal arts college:

Teachers, let me tell you, are born deceivers of the lowest sort, since what they want from life is impossible—time-freed, existential youth forever. It commits them to terrible deceptions and departures from the truth. And literature, being lasting, is their ticket.

Everything about the place was meant to be lasting—life no less than the bricks in the library and books of literature, especially when seen through the keyhole of their incumbent themes: eternal returns, the domination of man by machine, the continuing saga of choosing middling life over zesty death, on and on to a wormy stupor. Real mystery—the very reason to read (and certainly write) any book—was to them a thing to dismantle, distill and mine out into rubble they could tyrannize into sorry but more permanent explanations; monuments to themselves, in other words. (Ford, 1986, pp. 222–223)

There is good reason to suspect the motivations for and the basic desirability of temporal permanence. As discussed in previous chapters, the egoism alone of such a quest makes it problematic as a frame for any teacher's self-understanding. But it also fails even by its own logic; it is just not altogether clear why anyone should want it.

THE MAGIC OF RITUAL: *IN ILLO TEMPORE*

Nonetheless, I mean to argue that immortality and the attempt to achieve it still makes a great deal of sense. It is just that our first-glance conception of it is misguided. Because of our religious and cultural baggage, we tend to think of it as: (1) a personal matter involving the persistence of the soul or personality, and/or (2) a linear phenomenon involving temporal permanence. My view is that both (1) and (2) are deeply wrongheaded ways of thinking about immortality, though they are the most common ways we tend to think of it. It is hard *not* to think of it in these ways. Yet I would argue that when it is properly conceived, the desire for immortality *and its culmination* (I think it is possible to achieve it) are precisely flights *from* both (1) and (2). Frankly, and I hope that at this stage of the inquiry this much has been made clear, neither personal immortality in the traditional Judeo-Christian sense nor simply persisting through time onward to some senseless "end" hold much allure for me. What does hold some allure, though, is the possibility of becoming immortal *here and now* or, more properly, jumping ship outside of time altogether, escaping as did archaic humanity from Eliade's terror of history—the Sisyphean meaninglessness of the march of time. It seems to me that it just might still be possible to pull off such an escape. But one has to work at it.

One of the major themes in Eliade's writing is that a common element in archaic religions the world over—east, west, north, and south—is the centrality of what he calls the Great Time, the sacred time of beginnings, "in those days," *in illo tempore, ab origine*—the nostalgic, mythic age of gold (or some other incomparable precious-ness) in which the world was created and heroes, gods, and the like roamed the earth in direct communication with human beings. This is the "once upon a time" *par excellence*: the dreamtime, the days of yore—lost, as they say, "in the mists of time." For it has indeed been lost somehow, and as a result human beings feel themselves to be, as Eliade puts it, "'cut off' from 'something' powerful":

> "something" utterly *other* than himself, and at other times from an indefinable, timeless "state," of which he has no precise memory, but which he does however remember in the depths of his being: a primor-dial state which he enjoyed before Time, before History. This separation has taken the form of a fissure, both in himself and in the world. It was a "fall," not necessarily in the Judeo-Christian meaning of the term, but a fall nevertheless since it implies a fatal disaster for the human race and at the same time an ontological change in the structure of the World. (Eliade, 1965, p. 122)

Some great cataclysm (sin, flood, fire) separates human beings off from this primordial sacred realm and consigns them to the profane realm, with profane time. In this realm are possible rituals that "ap-proximate" those originary events *in illo tempore*, and in so doing evince a deep nostalgia and, above all, respond to an abiding fear of mortality and its concomitant historical mode of existence. The terror of history is precisely this: the sense of meaningless belonging to history as an irreversible timeflow, where everything is swept up and away, where nothing—including human beings, their aspirations, their culture—has enduring value. A fear of profane, linear time: "History . . . is a nightmare from which I'm trying to awake," as goes the famous line of Joyce's (1922/1986) Stephen Dedalus.

One might even speak of a "primitive ontology," in which the sacred Great Time is the primary reality upon which profane rituals model themselves and, ultimately, attempt to recapitulate. "An ob-ject or act becomes real only insofar as it imitates or repeats an arche-type" (Eliade, 1954, p. 34); the profane now-beads of historical time lack reality. Eliade, in fact, identifies Platonic idealism as having heavy residues of this archaic mentality:

> The distance between Plato and the primitive world is too obvious for
> words; but that distance does not imply a break in continuity. In this
> Platonic doctrine of Ideas, Greek philosophy renewed and re-valorized
> the archaic and universal myth of a fabulous, pleromatic *illud tempus*,
> which man has to remember if he is to know the *truth* and participate in
> *Being*. The primitive, just like Plato in his theory of *anamnesis* [i.e., learn-
> ing as recollection], does not attach importance to *personal* memories:
> only to myth, the exemplary History is of importance to him. . . . In
> Plato it is only the pre-existence of the soul in the timeless universe of
> Ideas that matters; and the *truth (aletheia)* is the remembrance of that
> impersonal situation (Eliade, 1960, pp. 52–53).

Archaic human beings (to generalize) seek via ritual to dip back into
that sacred time, not so unlike the Platonic immortality strategy of
linking up with that which is timeless and imperishable. In so doing
they attempt to *participate* in that sacred time and become godlike,
extratemporal. "In imitating the exemplary acts of a god or of a
mythic hero or simply by recounting their adventures, the man of an
archaic society detaches himself from profane time and magically
re-enters the Great Time, the sacred time" (Eliade, 1960, p. 23).

In contemporary life, we still have the broken shards of these
traditions, for example, in the pagan lineage of many holiday celebra-
tions, where the precise historical moment of Halloween, New
Year's, or Christmas is beside the point. (Christmas and Easter, in
fact, seem good illustrations of the Judeo-Christian attempt to hijack
archaic time-consciousness. Consider the historical status of the birth,
death, and resurrection of Jesus—presumed to be *real*, that is to say,
historical, events—as against that of the pagan elements retained in
the festivals supposed to "commemorate" those events: Santa Claus,
the Easter Bunny, and so forth. The historian's location of the "real"
Saint Nicholas is not nearly as interesting. One might rightly say that
Santa Claus is timeless, whereas Jesus is not.) Key here is the archaic
idea that ritual has the power to free one from historical time, to take
one into another realm, one somehow *more real* than what one inhab-
its every day. ("Yes, Virginia, there *is* a Santa Claus. Thank God! He
lives and he lives forever.")[1] The "method" of transport into this
other realm is the ritual "repetition of certain paradigmatic gestures,"
in which there is effected "an implicit abolition of profane time, of
duration, of 'history'; and he who reproduces the exemplary gesture
thus finds himself transported into the mythical epoch in which its
revelation took place" (Eliade, 1954, p. 35). These rituals occur at
certain special times, times at which the individual of an archaic culture would consider himself *truly himself*, notably when accomplish-

ing certain important acts like "alimentation, generation, ceremonies, hunting, fishing, war, work" (ibid.). And also, one might add, during teaching and learning, any instance of which might be seen as a repetition of some archetypal intergenerational transaction, when, say, the gods first taught human beings to plant, to hunt, to nurture, to make war and peace, to speak.

As discussed in earlier chapters, think for example of Telemachos' guide Mentor, mouthpiece of the goddess of wisdom, Athene. If I am mentoring someone, why could I not understand myself as repeating, reenacting, or, in some strong sense, re-creating that archetypal relation between Mentor and Telemachos—or whatever mythic prototype has richness and resonance for me given who and where I am? What prevents me from *becoming* Mentor? Why not live, in the words of one popular contemporary writer, "a mythic life" (Houston, 1996)? It does not seem unthinkable that pedagogical relationships might be reanimated along such lines, just as a Melanesian fisherman out at sea "becomes the hero Aori and is projected into mythical time, into the moment when the paradigmatic voyage took place," or just as Darius, King of Persia, "saw himself as a new Thraetona, the mythical Iranian hero who was said to have slain a three-headed monster," or as "the Pharaoh himself is assimilated with the god Re, conqueror of the dragon (Eliade, 1954, pp. 36–38)." Pick your hero or heroine for the occasion, and creatively (is there any other way?) retell or relive the myth in your own situation. These mythical prototypes give power, richness, and resolve to those who ritually summon them from the sacred, ahistorical time buried within collective memory. Back when Mother Nature was not an advertising slogan and epics lived larger than "literature."

We need to recapture these stories, especially the collectively told and enacted kind that have always bound human beings together. We need more old wives' tales. Nowhere is the need greater than in education, where the stories are daily growing shorter and sparser, more hastily told to fewer and fewer. As Neil Postman (1995) declares in precisely this context: "Without a narrative, life has no meaning. Without meaning, learning has no purpose. Without a purpose, schools are houses of detention, not attention" (p. 7). Our stories seem draining down the same sinkhole as have our gods and heroes. A blues guitar player friend of mine once told me that there was only One Blues Song that he and everybody else was playing over and over again. Maybe there is just One Teacher as well. What does she have to say? If we want to find out, we must want to hear her story.

My argument is that a "remythicization" of our own individual actions and cultural practices as teachers and learners promises a kind of immortality different from that informed by the Judeo-Christian historicization of experience—the parricidal successor to the archaic understandings Eliade lays out in such fascinating detail. This involves rejecting the linear, eschatologically derived picture of immortality as temporal permanence while at the same time embracing Eliade's (1958) more pagan archaic vision of immortality as life outside of profane time, a vision that we glimpse through the ritual reenactment of archetypal deeds and heroes—a projection into the Great Time, wherein by "its repetition, the act coincides with its archetype, and time is abolished" (p. 32). This should help give some positive content to the truism that "teaching is its own reward" for, in fact, *it is*. If it is possible to accomplish this, it might even go some way toward reanimating or, to use riskier language, reenchanting, even resacralizing an enterprise threatened at every turn by forces that would mechanize it out of existence. All we need is Eliade's archetype—the exemplary model or paradigm—the pivot around which our educational immortality bids must turn.

HERMENEUTICS AND THE RETRIEVAL OF MEANING: BACK TO SOCRATES

As hinted in previous chapters, I propose that "golden oldie" Socrates as the archetype-exemplar for contemporary education.[2] He has never gone out of style; we need, as we always have, another "back to Socrates" movement. The guiding Socratic educational ideal of seeking Truth but always in and through Others manages productively the tension between the two ideals, the moral parameters within which teaching and learning must reside. It hits that sweet spot, that fruitful tension giving rise to education in the rich sense toward which this book as a whole means to gesture.

I believe that if we as a culture truly took the "myth" of Socratic education seriously, as has been done only rarely in Western history, we could effect a veritable pedagogical renaissance that could pervade all of our educational institutions. This is because it would help place education where it belongs: at the center of our cultural agenda, where hearts and minds, adults and children, ancestors and progeny all meet. We could stand to think more about how education speaks to our deepest hopes and dreams, how these hopes and dreams evoke more than our narrow selves and are larger even than our own place and time, why those involved keep coming back for more, despite the enterprise's traditionally lowly, even ignominious, social status. It would not hurt, in short, to consider why *having been an educator*—yes, "just" that—promises comfort on one's death bed, that *memento mori* upon which all of us (will) lie. Getting a better grip on these things will help us as educators pull ourselves up by our own symbolic and moral bootstraps. Those bootstraps are there, waiting to be pulled. Need it be said that no one else can do the pulling but us? Like a toddler finally rising to stand, we can—if we wish and work for it—transport ourselves to a place that is new and joyous, though it has been there all along.

Fortunately, there is a fairly well-developed theory providing an additional lens through which to see what I am advocating: philosophical hermeneutics, as it has been advanced most notably by Hans-George Gadamer and modified by others. Gadamer's hermeneutics provides us with a way to "Socratize" our understanding of education, and in so doing it gives us the archetype and the ideational framework within which ritually to enact it.

In earlier centuries, hermeneutics had a fairly narrow meaning denoting the proper methods for the exegesis of biblical texts (this will be elaborated below), but thanks to Gadamer the term has come to have a much wider meaning as a general philosophical theory of how it is we come to understand a text, another person or culture, or, really, anything at all. Indeed, nowadays hermeneutics is more or less a fancy synonym for the word *interpretation*, or perhaps more broadly, *understanding*. In a sense that this section aims to clarify, all education involves hermeneutics (cf. Gallagher, 1992). For is there ever learning without interpretation? Without understanding? To the degree that it is an interpretive process, a serious philosophical inquiry into education must look deeply into the workings of that process, deep into moral and epistemological caverns where educational psychology or "learning theory" cannot go. Hermeneutics provides, in a phrase, the nuts and bolts of immortality and education or, if you like, some contemporary conceptual machinery for "updating" the elusive Socratic pedagogical ideal of harmonizing Truth and the Other.

One proper starting point for a discussion of hermeneutics and education is—where else?—with Plato and the Sophists. Contemporary philosophical hermeneutics is prefigured in Plato's famous response in the *Meno* to the sophistic problem of how any learning is possible at all. The problem—"Meno's Paradox"—is that if we do not, on the one hand, in any way know in advance what we are searching for it would be *ipso facto* impossible to recognize it. Yet on the other hand, if we already know, we would no longer be in a state of ignorance. Thus the search—learning itself—would be superfluous. Plato appeals to the myth of *anamnesis* to answer the dilemma: We somehow recollect a pure realm of essences or Ideas with which we were allegedly once upon a time in immediate contact. This acquaintance, though prior to all earthly experience, is the basis upon which subsequent understanding occurs (Gadamer, 1980, pp. 26f.).

Interestingly enough for present purposes, what is primarily at stake in this dialogue is the immortality of the soul (yet another instance in Plato where education and immortality are presented as wrapped tightly together), yet it is the epistemological doctrine of *anamnesis* that is most relevant here, as it foreshadows what Gadamer (following his mentor Heidegger) would later call, in the context of biblical exegesis, the "hermeneutical circle." For Gadamer, it is particularly instructive that Plato's "resolution" to Meno's paradox is a *mythic* one regarded by Socrates' interlocutors in the dialogue as a mere "half-proof" (ibid.). This is because the dialectic of whole and part—the "to-and-fro" of interpretation—must be generated by an initial projection (or, in terms consonant with the present discussion, an archetype) that, to avoid an infinite regress, must be grounded somewhere—if need be, in myth. And this is what Plato does: He grounds this projection in a myth that explains how all human knowledge is possible, but which is itself beyond mortal senses. Consider an example from another dialogue, the *Phaedo*: If I see two twigs of approximately the same size, I am entitled to judge them "equal" by virtue of my prior access to the very Idea of "Equal," which enables me to "see" the equality in the manifestly unequal specimens before me. Otherwise, since no two earthly things persist in this relation after all measurement is exhausted—you will never find two things *exactly* alike—there would be no way for me to form the concept. But since I am, albeit in a limited way, privy to the world of Ideas, my understanding has a basis upon which it can project toward worldly experiences (74b). From this otherworldly initial projection (gotten from before I was born and not completely washed away by the river of forgetfulness [*lethe*] upon my birth), I am able to revise and extend my notion of "equal" as I encounter things in the world that approximate the primal—mythic—purity to greater or lesser degrees.

This need for an initial projection that I am arguing the doctrine of *anamnesis* fulfills—and which, also, is a sort of epistemological analogue to Eliade's notion of the *illud tempus* archetype that finite mortals subsequently repeat through ritual—is present in what Gadamer calls the "prehistory" of romantic hermeneutics and its tradition of biblical exegesis. Only here the archetype is the God-written Bible, the precise meaning of which is spelled out in official Church dogma and mediated through the proper authorities. Conveniently, here the word of God Himself supplies the archetype—or at least that is how the whole package is sold. This provides a solid enough basis of interpretation because although it is mediated by human beings, it is in principle accessible to everyone (God might always speak to you) and it is in fact by and large regarded as universally valid (because, as was the case for over a millennium, there existed a community that shared certain presuppositions: Christendom). Individual biblical passages must be interpreted in this "direct" light and, where this fails, with attention to an elaborate hierarchy of commentators with greater or lesser degrees of authority. Not until the presumption of the Protestant Reformation that the Bible is a self-unified whole whose basic meanings can be accessed by *any individual* without mediation does the need for a specific art of interpretation arise in theology (see also Seebohm, 1992).

This prizing of the autonomy of the understanding, which was given further shape by the scientific-methodological ideals of the Enlightenment, is the context within which the first bona fide hermeneutical theorist, the nineteenth-century German philosopher and theologian Friedrich Schleiermacher, generalizes the need for hermeneutical techniques, for an "art" of the understanding. As Gadamer (1989b) writes:

> The art of understanding came under fundamental theoretical examination and universal cultivation because neither scripturally nor rationally founded agreement could any longer constitute the dogmatic guideline of textual understanding. Thus it was necessary for Schleiermacher to provide a fundamental motivation for hermeneutical reflection and so place the problem of hermeneutics within a hitherto unknown horizon. (p. 176)

This "unknown horizon" no longer consists simply in applying hermeneutical techniques to ambiguous passages in the Bible (this had already been done, for example, by the seventeenth-century Dutch philosopher Baruch Spinoza). Schleiermacher's great contribution was to extend the scope of hermeneutics to cover *any* form of discourse. No longer could the certainty of any sort of understanding be assumed, even interpersonal communication. If one needs techniques of understanding for the Bible, maybe one needs them for understanding other people as well. Schleiermacher writes:

> Very often in the middle of a private conversation I avail myself of hermeneutic operations if I am not satisfied with a customary degree of understanding but seek to discover how in my friend's reflections the transition from one thought to another has been made, or if I trace the opinions, judgments and aspirations connected with the fact that he expresses himself precisely so and not otherwise with regard to an object under discussion. (Schleiermacher, 1835/1977, p. 315)

Even among friends, the need for interpretation may arise at any time.

From the perspective of the history of hermeneutics, Schleiermacher's is the key move, and—filtered through the German philosophers Wilhelm Dilthey, Edmund Husserl, and Heidegger—Gadamer takes this widening-out of the hermeneutical situation as the basis for his general theory of human understanding. For Gadamer, all understanding—whether of a text or of another person—is interpretive. Whatever else it is and does, understanding moves in the abovementioned hermeneutic circle: not in the sense of the logician's *faux pas* of assuming what one sets out to prove, but rather as the precondition for any meaning whatsoever. This is a circle *productive* of meaning. To generate meaning from a text, for instance, one must always move around from whole to part and back again. The "whole" may be the language within which the text was written, the literary tradition to which it belongs, its historical circumstances, the biographical details of its author, and so on. Or it might be as spare as some point of view or predisposition with which one approaches the text, like "this is a classic," "a *New York Times* best-selling mystery" (and hence promising of excitement, a "page-turner"), "a boring, assigned textbook," "a book by a racist," and so on. This whole, then, provides the backdrop against which one gives significance to the part, say, to particular passages within the text, the individual work as it relates to the author's corpus, or developments in the book's genre. A simple analogy is with understanding an ambiguous word in a sentence. As any grade school teacher must constantly point out, if the meaning of a word is not immediately obvious, one should first look to its larger context. The newly appreciated meaning of the part (the word) then alters to a degree the meaning of the whole (the sentence), and so on, dialectically, *ad infinitum*. But when one is executing this whole-to-part meaning creation, one never escapes to any "outside"—even the dictionary only relates words to other words.

Gadamer thus takes an old interpretive tradition and extends it far beyond the narrow confines of the exegesis of sacred texts, though, in an important sense that Gadamer readily acknowledges, he is really only reviving the ancient problematic laid out in Plato's response to Meno's paradox. Gadamer claims that the basic whole-part circular structure characterizes *any* attempt to understand, whether the object of that understanding is a text, a natural phenomenon, or even another person. Moreover, this perspective highlights how mutual understanding among persons has at least one key thing in common with the biblical tradition: To generate the potentially fecund hermeneutical circle—to make meaning happen—one must come to the text or person with an initial attitude characterized by a certain acceptance, granting it a sort of provisional truth. Just like some discourse communities have considered the Bible to be true (however difficult it may be for us benighted sinners to decipher), in general the Other's claim is innocent until proven guilty, not unlike what the analytical philosopher Donald Davidson (1984) calls the "principle of charity," which provides a moral and epistemological rule for making sense of someone else. However difficult it may be, I must approach your claim with the attitude that it may well be true, as opposed to, say, merely being "interested" in how exotic you are, taking you with a grain of salt, knowing what "you people" are like, and so on. For if the text or person is "known" beforehand to be false, a very different sort of understanding ensues; one does not attend to the substantive truth of what is being said, but rather to the reasons the falsehood is uttered, the motives of the speaker, and the like. In a word, the hermeneutic circle is flattened, in the sense that no longer is the text or person allowed to generate the circle of understanding. Instead, it is generated by the interpreter's own presumption of falsehood regarding what is written or said.

One common example of this in educational research is the prevailing attitude of adopting a distant-observer stance when studying teachers—their beliefs and behaviors—rather than finding ways to inquire *along with them* about the meaning of what they do. One may of course learn all sorts of interesting and important things via this sort of research, but in doing so—in adopting the initial distancing stance—one blocks out whole areas that for Gadamer are bound to be epistemically and, certainly, morally richer. Imagine if Socrates approached his interlocutors by suggesting that he "study" their responses to his questions, how they act in certain situations, what their underlying motives were. He would then not be as open to the idea that the Other *may well know something that is true* and would instead be pursuing "his own" research agenda. Again: There is nothing necessarily wrong with this. It is just not the whole story; and often, in fact, more is hidden by it than revealed.

This is why Gadamer argues that what I am calling the distant-observer stance tends to be prohibitive of understanding in its deepest sense. No matter how difficult it may be, if one really desires to understand the Other, then one must attempt—at least as an initial gesture of goodwill—to bracket one's motivating biases and attend to the substantive truth claims of the text or person; one must maintain that initial attitude of openness. This does not mean, though, that one can or even ought to strive to eliminate completely one's own prejudices. On the contrary, Gadamer argues against the possibility or desirability of a neutral, nonprejudicial standpoint from which to "evaluate" the Other (this would place one right back into the distant-observer stance). We all have a perspective, a "horizon" that we bring to the interpretive situation. There is no way to get away from that. (In this vein, neither does understanding in Gadamer's sense arise by being "swept up" by the Other, as one might be by a charismatic orator or, in the context of pedagogy, by the sort of teacher who cultivates a "guru" persona.) The interpretive challenge is to maintain simultaneously the attitude of openness toward the text or person while also permitting, as best one can, one's own prejudices to rise to the surface so as to "put them at play." One must, in a way, *put oneself at risk*. Meaning is made when one places one's own perspective into play with someone else's, not by sitting safely in the box seats or mimicking a leader.

But all this is easier said than done. How are we to understand let alone effect this delicate and demanding balancing act, where one is both open to the claims of the Other yet not forgetful or silent about one's own prejudices, one's own situatedness? Gadamer (1976) compares this interpretive situation with a dialogue in which "a spirit rules, a bad one or a good one, a spirit of obdurateness and hesitancy or a spirit of communication and of easy exchange between I and Thou" (p. 66). The spirit emerging from the dialogue is in turn likened to a game, whose normative authority (i.e., the rules and principles to which participants adhere in order to be playing) has a priority over the individual players. Insofar as they enter the world of the game, no matter how heated or competitive the playing of it might actually become, players cede their private concerns to something larger than themselves, namely, to the game itself. Indeed,

> the very fascination of the game for the playing consciousness roots precisely in its being taken up into a movement that has its own dy-

namic. The game is underway when the individual player participates in full earnest, that is, when he no longer holds himself back as one who is merely playing, for whom it is not serious. Those who cannot do this we call men who are unable to play. (ibid.)

It might even be said that the game itself "takes over," becoming the master of the players, even while its very being depends upon those same players to play it. One does not give oneself over completely to the game, though, for this would mean committing the error of assuming a false neutrality that aims at bypassing the problems of interpretation altogether. One cannot enter the game as "no one." One always enters the game as someone with a history, with projects, prejudices, hopes, dreams, vices, and virtues. Again: One must maintain oneself in one's preunderstandings (there is no other option) while simultaneously opening oneself in Socratic fashion to the "call"—the substantive truth claim—of the Other, thereby putting those very same entrance-ticket prejudices at risk.

For Gadamer, the play analogy is ontologically significant because the interpretive dialogue that hermeneutic understanding establishes with its object gives rise to something independent of both the understanding and the object. It creates something new. As the prejudices of the interpreting consciousness are put into play with those of the object—as their horizons are "fused"—a common living language emerges.[3] Writ large, this symbolic meeting ground of tradition, which both depends upon individuals and structures their being-in-the-world, their experience in the widest possible sense, is largely what another of Gadamer's intellectual ancestors, the nineteenth-century German philosopher G. W. F. Hegel (1807/1977), had in mind by "Spirit" (*Geist*), which comes to know itself through a process of *Bildung* (the German word, especially in Hegel's sense, is difficult to translate: it may mean, among other things, "culture," "development," and/or "education"). As one commentator describes the process:

> Gadamer compares *Bildung* to a progressive *fusion of horizons* in which interpreter and tradition are elevated to participation in a higher universality. This fusion is at once the cancellation of both the parochial prejudices of the interpreter which impede access to the unique message of the tradition and the dead anachronisms implicit in the latter as well as the *preservation* and *extension* of what is common to both of them. The moment of cancellation results in a dual negation whereby both the being of the interpreter and the being of the tradition are altered. (Ingram, 1984, p. 70)

Unlike Hegel, however, Gadamer does not posit an end-state of absolute knowledge in which Spirit comes to know itself completely. His concept of experience is much more open-ended than Hegel's; it does not "progress" through the undergoing of stages but rather renders itself ever more open to new experiences. This is the true meaning of education for Gadamer; *Bildung* is a never-ending process of openness and a perpetual fusion of horizons—arising via dialogue's many forms—in which the learning never ends.[4]

As Gadamer (1989b) famously concludes the "Afterword" to his magnum opus *Truth and Method* (after some 579 pages!): "the ongoing dialogue permits no final conclusion. It would be a poor hermeneuticist who thought he could have, or had to have, the last word" (p. 579). The truly educated person—the true "hermeneuticist"—is "radically undogmatic" and ever open to the "experience that is made possible by experience itself" (ibid., p. 355). Such a person is open for education through intercourse with others as he undergoes a "continually recurring temptation to engage oneself in something or to become involved with someone" (Gadamer, 1989a, p. 26). The educated person is so "dialogically sensitive" that the mere *presence* of the Other (perhaps even to mind only) can help break up his biases and enlarge his vision; ideally, one always carries the Other along with one when one inquires, teaches, learns.

To make the notion of *Bildung* more concrete, Gadamer recasts it as a dialogue between interpreter and tradition in which the latter is experienced as a Thou (to borrow Martin Buber's (1923/1958) terminology). This point must be stressed: He is not saying that individuals such as teachers and students in every case ought to engage in an intersubjective give-and-take. (In fact, Gadamer argues explicitly against erecting dialogue in the usual sense as an overarching model for pedagogy.) Accordingly, sharing in this historically constituted conversation does not mean that I experience tradition as the opinion of some person or other, but rather that I am able to enter it as into a game made up of myself and other persons but not reducible to any of us. As much as anything does, it has a life of its own. The pedagogical ideal, then, is not exactly to establish zones of dialogue among students (though this may well be a good thing to do), but rather to *facilitate* a grander dialogue between students and their tradition(s)—whatever that tradition may happen to be. But it has to be *some* tradition, for whether we appreciate it or not, all of us are "worked on" by some tradition or other. If we let ourselves, we might even be surprised by what works on us. As Carl Jung (1959) once remarked: "A negro of the Southern States of America dreams in myths of

Grecian mythology and a Swiss grocer's apprentice repeats, in his psychosis, the vision of an Egyptian Gnostic" (p. 37).

A Gadamerian–Socratic teacher does not convert or proselytize but rather uses whatever means are morally acceptable to get students swept up in and carried away by *Bildung*, just as she herself must be. A teacher who is not "carried away" by something is no teacher at all, for it is in being carried away that one is moved to carry others away, too. As the British philosopher Michael Oakeshott (1989) once memorably put it: "This civilized inheritance, this world of meanings and understandings, will be transmitted only where it inspires the gratitude, the pride, and even the veneration of those who already enjoy it, where it endows them with an identity they esteem, and where it is understood as a repeated summons rather than a possession, an engagement rather than an heirloom" (p. 67). The joy in this "game" lies in *passing it on*, just as catching and throwing are more fun than holding. When a child holds the ball for too long, she must be taught to give it up. When a tradition is regarded as a possession, it ceases to speak; its would-be guardians bind and gag it. But hearing that tradition—and being heard in it—are what it is all about. It is a dialogue whose scale is much larger than is usually imagined. And so, just as one should not be surprised if in the course of a conversation one is asked something by one's interlocutor, *Bildung*—like any dialogue partner—may ask something of its teachers *in return*. This, I think, is what Oakeshott means; it is Socratic through and through.

And Gadamer models this edifying give-and-take and its "structure of openness" precisely upon Socratic dialogue, which is driven by a sincere questioning into some subject matter and where dialogue partners set out neither to outwit, outargue, generically "explain," nor divine the motivations of one another. (It is quite possible that someone "practicing the art of dialectic" will even come off worse in the eyes of those observing the exchange.) The basic conditions for such a conversation are like those of understanding itself because both exhibit, in the words of one scholar of Gadamer, the tension "between presuming the truth claims of one's object and adapting them—even if unconsciously—according to the traditions of one's time and place" (Warnke, 1987, p. 100). The hermeneutic circle that constitutes the living being of tradition is thus well described as a dialogue or conversation between initial preunderstandings or prejudices in which they fuse and are fused into something more than they were by themselves beforehand. That is what a teacher tries to get going: that fusing of students' own backgrounds and interests with the ongoing tradition that precedes them and will, lest it be forgotten, outlive them all. This is how education manufactures culture (and vice versa).

Conditions for this fusion are optimized when the interlocutors possess that attitude of openness reminiscent of the Socratic profession of ignorance ("The truth keeps eluding me, but maybe you know something of it: Let us search for it together.") Through dialogue, I recognize both my own and my partner's (remember—this "partner" could be a person, a text, or something more encompassing, such as some subject matter, even an entire tradition of thought) finitude and fallibility as we foreground each others' hidden assumptions and beliefs. In other words, a genuinely questioning attitude highlights one's situatedness and hence the contingency of one's opinions; one learns that one does not know—the "most extreme negativity of doubt" (Gadamer, 1989b, p. 362). In this state of readiness for understanding the thing itself, prejudices may be put into play upon a field wherein persons, to use Hegel's (1807/1977) phrase, for the first time "*recognize* themselves as *mutually recognizing* one another" (p. 112, emphasis in original). This mutual recognition is manifest in the intersubjective substratum that an authentic dialogue discloses:

> Coming to an understanding in conversation presupposes that the partners are ready for it and that they try to allow for the validity of what is alien and contrary to themselves. If this happens on a reciprocal basis and each of the partners, while holding to his own ground simultaneously weights the counter-arguments, they can ultimately achieve a common language and a common judgment in an imperceptible and non-arbitrary transfer of viewpoints (Gadamer, 1989b, p. 388).

This emergent common language is nothing less than the "*Logos*, which is neither mine nor yours and which therefore so far supersedes the subjective opinions of the discussion partners that even the leader of the discussion always remains the ignorant one" (ibid.).

The resultant edifying dialogue therefore "always involves rising to a higher universality that overcomes not only our own particularity but also that of the other" (ibid., p. 305). This ceaseless overcoming is a process of *Bildung*, which is not something autonomous subjects "do," but is rather more like something done *with* them; we "fall into" conversation and are "swept away" as by something with a life of its own: "Understanding or its failure is like an event that happens to us. Thus we can say that something was a good conversation or that it was ill fated. All this shows that a conversation has a spirit of its own, and that the language in which it is conducted bears its own truth within it—i.e., that it allows something to "emerge" which henceforth exists" (ibid., p. 383). To the extent, then, that *Bildung* happens *to* us, it would be imprecise to characterize Gadamer's philosophical hermeneutics as prescriptive, that is, as providing a code of dialogical conduct to which individuals ought to adhere (this is an important difference between Gadamer's approach and the influential—in education and elsewhere—"communicative ethics" of Jurgen Habermas; see Burbules, 1993). Instead, given the explicit analogy with the homecoming of Hegelian Spirit, it seems more appropriate to describe it as *teleological* (Ingram, 1984, p. 68).

But it is indeed an odd sort of teleology that, again unlike Hegel's (or Christianity's), provides no guaranteed end-point, "rational" or otherwise. For what sense is one to make of a goal that has no end? An end that is *end*-less? It seems a contradiction in terms. I would suggest, though, that we view Gadamer's philosophical hermeneutics—his explication of the Socratic dialectic's synthesis of Truth and the Other—through the lenses provided by Eliade's account of ritual as an escape from profane (linear) time. Here, an end-less end makes perfect sense: *as an immortality bid.* But, as outlined toward the beginning of this chapter, it is one dedicated to something other than temporal permanence: an attempt to escape time altogether, and with it Eliade's terror of history, by catapulting the teacher–learner—that ritualizer of the quest for Truth through similarly inquiring and suffering Others—into the onrunning stream of *Bildung.* Again: The movement is from the everlasting to the eternal. *That* is the payoff: being part of that eternal stream, dissolving into it, taking it on and being taken by it. *Being there.*

It turns out that "having an influence" as a teacher, or "being influenced" as a student (all of us teachers are always both), is, in fact, after all, a means to an end: immortality. This is just as was feared, it would seem, back in the critique of Plato's "spiritualized egocentrism." But not quite. Really, not at all: Following Gadamer's game-playing analogy, it is not exactly *my* immortality that I am pursuing. "My immortality" is the real contradiction in terms, for immortality consists precisely in the severing of the two terms, in the dissociation of the "my" from the "immortality." This is what happens when one enters, or I should say, *becomes Bildung.* It is through the creative appropriation of tradition that we become immortal, playing the game of the *logos,* letting it play us. In the singular enterprise known as education (there are as many ways to play the *Bil-*

dung-immortality game as there are ways to make culture, from that One Blues Song to the mathematician at Princeton, to a parent keeping his or her child "on the right track"), this means pulling off that most challenging of all navigational feats: keeping in sight these twin beacons Truth and Other, not running aground on either's shore, but instead letting them guide one's voyage to the Center: to the Sacred Mountain, the Gate of the Gods, the Bond of Heaven and Earth, the *omphalos*, Jerusalem, Golgotha (Eliade, 1954, pp. 12–17). Back to "those days," *in illo tempore*. We have all been there; and we can go back, again and again. "It is here! It is here!" says the Tantric aphorism (Campbell, 1949, p. 189); it is yours and mine for the taking.

SUMMARY

To summarize: In the above-described edifying, tradition-forming, revising and conserving dialogue—Hegelian Spirit conversing with itself—arises *Bildung*, which I see as education's Alpha and Omega, and as such the key to educational immortality. For, again, *Bildung* means development, culture, and education all rolled into one: the creative, yet ritual (re)enactment, even "repetition," of archetypal traditions (Eliade) that give rise to something larger and beyond the individuals doing the enacting. Gadamer's hermeneutics provides a grand metaphor for how educational immortality bids proceed, their mechanics: through tradition, through Others, always seeking Truth, cognizant of individual and collective human limitation, fallibility and, ultimately, mortality and its negation. Educators are well situated for achieving immortality (though not uniquely so) whenever and wherever we can make a harmony of the tension between Truth and the Other. This is our Holy Grail. In finding this harmony—for a minute, an hour, a year or two, or twenty—we can "make it," back to that place archaic humanity routinely summons via ritual, where "mine" dissolves into "thine," future into past, and earth into heaven. Here lies a wellspring of meaning and sustenance, right here, hidden in the day-to-day. It is the rose in the cross of the present.[5] Not beyond, or above, or at the end of the rainbow, but right under our very noses. There are teachers-and-learners who are, right now, *at this very moment*, immortal. They know it. We know it. Let us learn how to celebrate it, too.

CHAPTER 5

Further Questions

The eternal gods
Are full of life for ever; but unto death
A man also
Can retain the best in mind
And crown his life with it.

—*Freidrich Hölderlin (1798/1990)*

Since the Socratic myth would be ill served by "conclusions" in the usual sense, I will close with two further questions. They are honest ones, and I do not pretend to be able to answer them fully.

QUESTION 1

Myth is strong medicine and as such can harbor danger. Only a cursory look at this century shows the horrific uses to which it can be put: from Nazi "blood and soil," to Balkans-style "ethnic cleansing," to the homegrown bizarre mix of white supremacy and apocalyptic Christianity that continues to attract adherents on the far right (K. Stern, 1996). In the present context, this concern is magnified by the disturbing political views of several of the theorists from whom I have drawn most heavily: Plato, Heidegger, and Eliade.[1]

Heidegger, for example, was apparently strongly drawn in by one of the most seductive—and deeply reactionary—mythmakers of our time: the German literary figure Ernst Jünger. Jünger's prowar novels (e.g., *The Storm of Steel*, hauntingly echoed in Nazi propagandist Josef Goebbels's exhortations for a "steely romanticism") were widely read during the 1920s and 1930s in Germany, even by schoolchildren (Herf, 1984). Like many other World War I veterans and right wing romantics, Jünger thought he had glimpsed authentic community amidst the battlefield trenches; the *Fronterlebnis* became a guiding image of a *Gemeinschaft* (i.e., authentic community) to be rekindled within the fragmented and alienated *Gesellschaft* (i.e., fragmented society) of bourgeois (Weimar) society (ibid., pp. 70–71). This would be accomplished by a new type of "heroic man" called forth by modern technological warfare, a "steely romantic" able to regard the death and destruction around him—even his own—as a purely aesthetic or mythical phenomenon, unburdened by ethical and political worries. As Jünger puts it, "the modern force field surrounding the *Gestalt* of the worker destroys all alien obligations . . . " (Jünger, 1972, p. 271).

Consistent with this mythic eclipsing of the moral realm, Jünger's "magical realism" is rife with passages like the following:

> Once again: the ecstasy. The condition of the holy man, of great poets and of great love is also granted to those of great courage. The enthusiasm of manliness bursts beyond itself to such an extent that the blood boils as it surges through the veins and flows as it foams through the heart. . . . It is an intoxication beyond all intoxication, an unleashing that breaks all bonds. It is a frenzy without caution or limits, comparable only to the forces of nature. There [in combat] the individual is like a raging storm, the tossing sea and the roaring thunder. He has melted into everything. He rests at the dark door of death like a bullet that has reached its goal. And the purple waves crash over him. For a long time he has no awareness of the transition. It is as if a wave slipped back into the flowing sea. (Jünger, 1922, p. 57; see also Zimmerman, 1990, pp. 46–93)

Needless to say, this is a sickening quote, and anyone interested in advocating a "mythicization" of anything is responsible for an explanation of how myths like Jünger's "storm of steel," "the total mobilization [for the war effort] of the worker-soldier," and so forth are out of bounds. Myth—to use a myth—is a Pandora's box. And if one of the greatest minds of this century can be seduced by such rot as Jünger's, I suppose anyone can. Immunity, it seems, is not to be developed on account of intelligence, philosophical acumen, or even a disposition to ask and keep on asking the most basic questions. Who would deny Heidegger—yes, Heidegger the Nazi—this latter?

It is thus with a great deal of suspicion that I read Postman (1995): "Even if a narrative places one in hell, it is better to be there than nowhere. To be nowhere means to live in a barren culture, one that offers no vision of the past or future, no clear voice of authority, no organizing principles. In such a culture what are schools for? What *can* they be for?" (pp. 12–13). Better to be "in hell . . . than nowhere"? Surely this is excessively hyperbolic; one can go wrong with myth—more wrong, perhaps, than one can go in any other way. If a choice were necessary, I for one would have no doubt about opting for anomic, directionless, even spiritually empty schools rather than for Nazi schools that are *Gemeinschaft*-laden, blood and soil directioned, and otherwise brimming over with myth and meaning. It may be a choice between hanging or drowning, but even so: There are, after all, better and worse ways to die.

All of this is by way of suggesting that the Eliade-inspired mythic conception of education as immortality, with Socrates as archetype, must somehow maintain its critical faculties. This is the main reason why what I am advocating is different from a nostalgic return to the precritical innocence alleged to obtain in archaic cultures' narratives: the romantic taking leave of one's senses characteristic of a consciousness prone to mimesis (i.e., to being swept up in a story so intensely as to identify oneself with the protagonists—a phenomenon also part and parcel of the flight from the terror of history).[2] It may well be, as the political theorist and U.S. presidential adviser William Galston (1989) has remarked, that "the greatest threat to children in modern liberal societies is not that they will believe in something too deeply, but that they will believe in nothing very deeply at all" (p. 101). It does not follow from this, however, that *any* convictions are to be welcomed. Hence the bind: How does one separate the wheat from the chaff? Which convictions, myths—or whatever "stories"—are worth embracing, and which are not? The answer involves, it seems to me, including some conception of critical consciousness, the ability to deliberate rationally among options—even options for how to understand oneself—as they are laid before one. The difficulty, though, is that the ability to deliberate rationally presupposes an ability to distance oneself from the options upon which one is deliberating, even if only temporarily, so as to weigh the desirability of one's choice. But this same critical distance prevents one from entering into the mimetic state needed to get a full-bodied myth going in the first place. Once the critical cat is out of the bag, can it be put back in? Should it ever be? And even if it could (and should) be, how could it remain the same old cat?

For critical rationality seems inherently corrosive of myth—and vice versa. Simon Schama (1995), in his remarkable book on landscape and nature myths, puts the problem as well as anyone:

> So how much myth is good for us? And how can we measure the dosage? Should we avoid the stuff altogether for fear of contamination or dismiss it out of hand as sinister and irrational esoterica that belong

only in the unsavory margins of "real" (to wit, our own) history? Or do we have to ensure that a *cordon sanitaire* of protective irony is always securely in place when discussing such matters? . . .

The real problem . . . is whether it is possible to take myth seriously on its own terms, and to respect its coherence and complexity, without becoming morally blinded by its poetic power . . . without either losing ourselves altogether in total immersion or else rendering the subject "safe" by the usual eviscerations of Western empirical analysis. (p. 134)

Schama goes on to advise that, even as we recognize all of the above, if we refuse to take myth seriously, we "impoverish our understanding of our shared world," as we do also if we "concede the subject by default to those who have no critical distance from it at all, who apprehend myth not as a historical phenomenon but as an unchallengeable perennial mystery" (ibid.). In the wrong hands, our antidote could become our poison. This problem is particularly acute in education. How can I advocate, as many have, a pedagogical practice centered around the production of meaning, meanings that are inescapably over and above particular individuals, that are "wild" and therefore beyond anyone's control in an important sense, while also wanting as an educator for my charges to think for themselves? Children of Enlightenment on romanticism's dark mountain of storm and stress? Can they find their way? Can that way make pedagogical sense?

QUESTION 2

From the pyramids at Giza on, the quest for immortality has often been associated with elitist and authoritarian politics. I have tried to gesture toward a kind of immortality that need not be implicated with anything of the kind. But as Bauman (1992) starkly declares, "immortality is ultimately a *social relation*" (p. 55, emphasis in original). More, he continues, the "hope of immortality was preceded by, and founded in, earthly privilege" (ibid., p. 65). Take Plato's *Republic*, for example, where political power derives in a striking way from the Guardians' proximity to the eternal world of true Forms or Ideas. Here, the right to rule is in a way founded upon an immortality claim, a species of claim traditionally the province of the privileged. Immortality has simply not been available to the masses in the same way it has been to the elite. Immortality seems as implicated in inequality as it could be. Bauman extends the point:

In short—though the question of the meaning of life was eminently 'askable,' the ways to the construction of such meaning were, for the 'masses,' theoretically off-limits and practically beyond reach. The elite had evidently arrogated all recognized means appropriate to rendering life 'meaningful'—endorsed by the authority of lasting values, referring to something infinite and eternal, and thereby transcending the ephemerality of transient bodily existence. The elite reserved for its own use all the 'officially listed' roads leading to individual immortality. 'The masses,' already depersonalized in their earthly life, had been by the same token expropriated from the means of immortality production. (ibid., p. 103)

The "privatized" immortality championed by organized religion thus provided a cheap otherworldly substitute: a mass ontological sham perpetrated upon the masses, who, upon being denied the real immortality of terrestrial works and deeds, attempt to locate it in chimeras such as heaven, their souls, and so forth—an ersatz equal opportunity immortality that grew to be thought of as the real thing. Not only, then, might the ideal seem tainted by its provenance, but the traditional substitutions for it are even worse: variations on the noble lie even more elaborate than Plato envisaged.

Is it possible, then, that the kind of immortality I am advancing here might play into the hands of elites only too happy to deflect the masses' attention away from their material circumstances? Would, say, teachers who "bought" my idea that immortality is central to the enterprise of education be more likely to retreat into monkish isolation and eschew worldy affairs? Would they burn their union cards and quit caring about politics, the quest for immortality being their opiate?

I think it is indeed difficult to predict how such an idea might play out politically. I would hazard a thought or two, though. It seems to me that a focus on immortality might just as easily invigorate political commitment as lead to quiescence.[3] If one were truly committed to educational immortality in this book's sense, one would also be committed to defeating obstacles to that immortality: forces that do not permit one to teach Truth (e.g., obnoxious curriculum directives), that impede one's proximity to the Other (e.g., factory-style schools, a lack of material resources for all of one's students), that stand in the way of cultivating the kind of learning community necessary to sustain the ritual enactment of mythic archetypes (e.g., the batch processing of students, the reduction of teaching-and-learning to quantitative measurement). Along such lines, there seems to me a wealth of political work for teacher-immortals to do, and most of it, I think, dovetails nicely with a commitment to democratic education broadly conceived. And besides, to be fair, let it not be forgotten that this same question may be asked of *anyone* with a political agenda: What, in the end, fires *your* political engagement? And what fires *that*? Who has an easy answer?

As with any moral or political ideal, education as immortality may fall victim to its own peculiar corruptions—though I hope to have spoken successfully to the most common forms that corruption might take. Accordingly, wariness is always recommended, as in all human undertakings. Yet it seems to me a risk worth taking: Education is—as it must be—epistemologically, morally, and spiritually dangerous; and therefore something about it must surpass even the most humane political program. The politics of education as immortality are probably always to a degree undecided and aporetic. Maybe this is as it should be. As it *has* to be.

Notes

CHAPTER 1

1. *Symposium* 210–212. Here I follow a common line of interpretation, perhaps defended best by Gregory Vlastos (1981), who holds that the Platonic view of love "does not provide for the love of whole persons, but only for love of that abstract version of persons which consists of the complex of their best qualities. . . . When loved as congeries of valuable qualities, persons cannot compete with abstractions of universal significance, like schemes of social reform or scientific and philosophical truths, still less with the Idea of Beauty in its sublime transcendence, 'pure, clear, unmixed, not full of human flesh and color and other mortal nonsense' (*Symposium* 211e). The high climactic moment of fulfillment—the peak achievement for which all lesser lovers are to be 'used as steps'—is the farthest removed from affection for concrete human beings" (pp. 31–32). Yet this does not suggest that there need be anything exactly crude about this form of "using" someone else; if nothing else, it is as refined an exploitation as there could be, and perhaps even a mutually beneficial one. Indeed, as Vlastos himself notes (ibid., 40), Platonic lovers may "walk together in a life of shining happiness and, when the time comes, they shall grow wings together because of their love" (*Symposium* 256d). For an alternative picture, relying upon evidence from Xenophon's portrait of Socrates, see David K. O'Connor (1994), where it is argued that Socrates is "erotically *attracted* by his associates because he enjoys improving them through bringing them to acknowledge their ignorance" (p. 179). In O'Connor's view, the interaction itself may have a "kick" sufficient to obviate the need for any external motivation. I am indebted here to Professor O'Connor's helpful criticisms of an earlier draft of this paper.

2. The French feminist philosopher Luce Irigaray (1994), in her compelling discussion of Diotima's speech in the *Symposium*, makes a distinction between the first part of the speech, where love is "the mediator of a becoming with no objective other than becoming," and the second part, where "she used love itself as a *means*" (p. 194). Irigaray favors the former conception, as do I.

3. They also trained teachers, who in turn became Sophists themselves (see Kerferd, 1981, p. 17).

4. The die-hard pragmatist will object that our mathematician's psychic-aesthetic "satisfaction" is but a practical consequence of his mathematical

activity. This is true but trivial. It drains the term *practical* of any meaning at all, as pragmatists who overextend themselves are wont to do.

5. The quotation is from remarks delivered at the official celebration of Max Planck's 60th birthday. Einstein continues: "The supreme task of physics is to arrive at those universal elementary laws from which the cosmos can be built up by pure deduction. There is no logical path to these laws; only intuition, resting on sympathetic understanding, can lead to them. . . . The longing to behold [cosmic] harmony is the source of the inexhaustible patience and perseverance with which Planck has devoted himself . . . to the most general problems of science. . . . The state of mind that enables a man to do work of this kind is akin to that of the religious worshipper or the lover; the daily effort comes from no deliberate intention or program, but straight from the heart" (p. 222).

6. Plato seems to hold that knowing the Good will somehow thereby enjoin one actively to seek its sublunary instantiation. One somehow gets more of it this way, on the analogy of being "pregnant" (with Truth). This is the view of Diotima's *Symposium* speech: One gets more of what one values by propagating it. Yet why should this be so? Why should knowing the Good—or any other Form—involve activism of any sort beyond the "activity" of knowing it? To put it in another way: If one is indeed grasping the Infinite, of what worth is yet another finite manifestation? Terence Irwin (1977) explains that "throughout Plato assumes that the philosopher's knowledge of the Forms will create the desire to express his knowledge in actions" (p. 237). The key word here is "assumes."

CHAPTER 2

1. Plato's often-used notion of opposites is notoriously obscure. Why should everything have one and only one opposite? (Cf. *Protagoras* 332c–333b.) Consider Aristotle's notion of virtue as a mean between an excess and a defect. Courage, for example, is the mean between cowardice (defect) and rashness (excess). But which is the "opposite" of courage? Why not both? Some argue it is impossible for Plato not to have recognized this and that therefore he is intentionally placing this bad argument into Socrates' mouth for other purposes. (See Melling, 1987, p. 44.)

2. From the mountain of commentary on this part of the *Phaedo*, I have found especially helpful discussions in P. Stern (1993, pp. 54f.), Patterson (1965, pp. 22–32); and McPherran (1994, passim).

3. Paxton (1990) provides some historical context to my personal observations, as well as some suggestive linkages with the discussion of the Greeks, in his splendid book: "The Jews' experience of exile in the sixth century B.C. and the struggle against Greek cultural and political hegemony in the second century led to the erosion of the ancient conception of a shadowy after life in the She'ol and the first expressions of expectations of a

personal judgment and the resurrection of the just at the end of time.
. . . The growing interest in the fate of the soul in the afterlife among both
Jews and pagans accompanied a shift away from the fear of the dead to
fear of their welfare in the afterlife" (pp. 19–20). There is a conception of
immortality—life after death—in most forms of Judaism, but its precise nature
is a matter of ongoing discussion. One expression of the difference between
Judaism and traditional Christianity is found in an official platform statement
of Reform Judaism (Pittsburgh, 1885): "We assert the doctrine that the soul
is immortal, founding this belief on the divine nature of the human spirit,
which forever finds bliss in righteousness and misery in wickedness. *We reject
as ideas not rooted in Judaism, the beliefs both in bodily resurrection and in Gehenna
and Eden [Hell and Paradise] as abodes for everlasting punishments and rewards"*
(Quoted in Olan, 1971, p. 96; emphasis added).

4. This practice may be rooted in hygiene: Bodies decomposed rapidly
in the heat of Palestine (Paxton, 1990, p. 21).

5. This is but one minor example among many used by Horkheimer and
Adorno (1972, pp. 47–48, n.5). One of the more extended examples is how
Odysseus has his crew stop up their ears in order to pass by the beautiful yet
deadly song of the Sirens. The crew must simply row without noticing anything but their immediate labor, the task at hand, while Odysseus has himself
strapped to the mast so he cannot get away. The crew thus becomes "practical" while Odysseus, in order to gain control, must immobilize himself (pp.
34–37). They summarize: "Mankind, whose versatility and knowledge becomes differentiated with the division of labor, is at the same time forced
back to anthropologically more primitive stages, for with the technical easing
of life the persistence of domination brings about a fixation of the instincts by
means of heavier repression. Imagination atrophies . . . adaptation to the
power of progress involves the progress of power, and each time anew brings
about those degenerations which show not unsuccessful but successful progress to be its contrary. The curse of irresistable progress is irresistable regres-
sion" (pp. 35–36).

6. Herf (1984) makes a convincing case that Nazism represents a *lack* of
enlightenment rather than an excess.

7. Bluebond-Langer (1980) documents the heart-rending fact that children facing death (e.g., the terminally ill) are strongly attracted to the "sad
parts" in E. B. White's (1952) classic *Charlotte's Web*.

8. Enzensberger (1993) has remarked that on the global scale the only
thing worse than being exploited by multinational corporations is *not* being
exploited by them. He calls this the problem of "extra people" (p. 25). See
also Blacker (1996).

9. This very scenario was the premise of the major motion picture *The
Doctor*, starring William Hurt (Haines, 1991). Not that this medical stance
may not achieve a high level of refinement, as in Nuland's (1994) riveting
How We Die. For a decidedly odd—even macabre—attempt by a journalist to
"get close" to death, see Lesy (1989).

10. See the first section of Gadamer (1989b) for an influential extended

critique of the isolation and nonrootedness of the contemporary artist (pp. 1-169).

11. As Garland (1985) notes, the "epitaph on the Athenian dead at Potidaia in 432 B.C., for example, states that 'ether [*aither*] received their *psuchai*, but earth their bodies.' A fourth-century inscription from the Peiraios reads: 'The moist *aither* holds the *psyche* and proud spirit of Eurymachos, but this grave holds his body'" (p. 75).

12. Garland (1985) also cautions, while commenting on the picture of the soul given by Plato's Socrates in the *Phaedo*: "It must be stressed that this notion of the *psuchē* as capable of being corrupted by earthly desires is unlikely to have been shared by many classical Greeks" (p. 19).

13. Plato's views are found in the *Phaedo, Gorgias, Republic* and elsewhere. See also McPherran (1994, passim) and Patterson (1965, pp. 126–127).

14. In the following discussion, I attempt to avoid the historical question of what influence Platonic doctrine may have had (or not had) upon subsequent Hellenistic thinkers such as Epicurus. I am merely trading upon what seems to me a limited conceptual affinity—a much weaker claim, but one that provides an important bridge to issues of pedagogical significance. To be sure, there is a case to be made for direct influence, since Xenocrates, a successor (after Speusippus) to Plato as head of the Academy, is reported to have "exalted" the ideal. (See Barnes, 1988, p. 365.)

15. Among Aristotle's (1984) discussions of slavery, see *Politics* 1254a14–17: "We see what is the nature and office of a slave; he who is by nature not his own but another's man, is by nature a slave; and he may be said to be another's man who, being a slave, is also a possession. And a possession may be defined as an instrument of action, separable from the possessor."

16. See, for example, Dewey (1916, pp. 69–110). A contemporary statement of this theme is skillfully presented in the context of a critique of Jean Piaget in Matthews (1994, pp. 10–40).

17. This does one better the notorious claim made during the 1980s by the Reagan administration that for nutritional purposes, ketchup should be counted as a vegetable. In this vein, Rodd (1992) reports that "McDonald's nutritionist Patricia Baird recently confessed to the *Boulder Daily Camera*, 'I don't have any idea in the world what is a 'healthy food'''" (p. 276).

18. As Weinberg (1993) laments: "But now we are stuck. The years since the mid-1970s have been the most frustrating in the history of elementary particle physics. We are paying the price of our own success: theory has advanced so far that further progress will require the study of processes at energies beyond the reach of existing experimental facilities" (p. 4).

19. See Aristotle, *Nicomachean Ethics* 1177a19–1177b26, where it is argued that the contemplative life is superior because it seeks no end outside itself. Interestingly enough in the present context, concerning this form of life he adds: "But such a life would be too high for man; for it is not in so far as he is man that he will live so, but in so far as something divine is present in him;

and by so much as this is superior to our composite nature is its activity superior to that which is the exercise of the other kind of excellence. If Intellect is divine, then, in comparison with man, the life according to it is divine in comparison with human life. But we must not follow those who advise us, being men, to think of human things, and, being mortal, of mortal things, but must, so far as we can, make ourselves immortal, and strain every nerve to live in accordance with the best thing in us; for even if it be small in bulk, the much more does it in power and worth surpass everything" (1177b27-1178a1).

CHAPTER 3

1. The famous example of this from Continental philosophy is Edmund Husserl's (1976) claim that we are never just "conscious" but always "conscious-of" something or other. I never just "hear," for example, but I hear a car door slam, a bird sing, my own breathing. Perception is always, so to speak, "in-the-world."

2. Hannah Arendt (1958) argues that this is one element of the genius of Christianity: Through the notion of forgiveness, it promises to lift the great weight of responsibility for the ever-expanding consequences flowing from our actions, "constantly releasing men from what they have done unknowingly" (p. 240).

3. I am indebted to Tronto (1993), which contains an extremely lucid and thoughtful account and critique of the relationship between Kohlberg and Gilligan (pp. 61-97).

4. Noddings (1992) herself acknowledges her debt in this regard to Heidegger, though she does not really engage his actual views (p. 15). Though highly (and justifiably) critical of Heidegger in many respects, Tronto (1993) also recognizes Heidegger's primacy regarding care, mostly in footnotes, where, in an otherwise fine and careful book, she unfortunately refers throughout to "*Zorg*," where she means *Sorge*, the German term (p. 182, 207). I mention this only because it underscores how care theorists, though often citing his authority, seem not really to have read Heidegger yet.

5. My critique of care theory was inspired by and remains indebted to Kymlicka (1990), pp. 238-292.

6. Some care theorists argue more circumspectly merely for the inseparability of justice and care, as opposed to the latter's priority—a view more consistent with my own. (See, e.g., Baier, 1995; Callan, 1992; Okin, 1989a, 1989b; Tronto, 1993). Baier (1995) writes: "It is clear, I think, that the best moral theory has to be a cooperative product of women and men, has to harmonize justice and care" (p. 57).

7. Michael Lind (1995) writes, "This approach replaces one kind of pious fraud with another . . . from all the attention given Crispus Attucks, one would never guess that the overwhelming majority of black Americans who

fought in the War of Independence fought *against* the United States on behalf of their freedom—and the first Great Emancipator, King George III of England. Rather than reflecting a really fresh look at American history, the tokenist approach parallels the Multicultural regime in co-opting representatives of aggrieved groups—a black American here, a white woman there—to shore up an otherwise unchanged structure'' (p. 358).

8. Cf. Asa Hilliard's ''African-American Baseline Essays,'' which according to Schlesinger (1992) have inspired Afrocentric curricula in several major U.S. school district (pp. 69-72). Lest any reader feel I am hereby allying myself with a conservative political agenda (which I am not), this same critique has been launched perhaps most effectively from those with left-wing sympathies. From the mountain of sources on this topic, see, from the center, the sometimes overly hyperbolic journalist Richard Bernstein (1994) and, more solidly from the left, T. Gitlin (1995). See especially Gitlin's depressing account of the mobbish identity politics deployed in Oakland, California, against the progressive UCLA historian and textbook writer Gary Nash's work (pp. 7-36). I myself witnessed a similar thrashing of Nash at the annual conference of the National Coalition of Educational Activists in Toledo, Ohio during this same period, the early 1990s.

9. Levine's (1992) interesting and fair-minded review of both Bernal's (1987) book and the debate surrounding it—entitled ''The Use and Abuse of *Black Athena*''—concludes by making in compelling fashion precisely my point regarding the teacher's inescapable obligation to Truth. While strongly sympathetic with Bernal's antiracism, she notes: '' . . . as a classicist and teacher of the very groups (African Americans at Howard and Jews at Bar-Ilan) whose contributions to 'the glory that was Greece' allegedly had been slighted in the historical record, I was above all morally compelled to know whether Bernal's story was not only riveting but true'' (p. 460). For a more polemical critique of Bernal, see Lefkowitz (1996).

10. A more sophisticated argument for politicizing the curriculum—one to which I am sympathetic—is based not on students' ''self-esteem'' but on their need to confront more forthrightly the actual conditions—social, political, economic, and so forth—that are oppressing them. See, for example, Kanpol and Yeo (1995): ''We have always contended that this form of pedagogy, guided by this philosophy, is good when it builds self-esteem and challenges positivistic truths. Unfortunately, in many inner-city schools, such holistic educational practices often become reduced to so-called feel-good teaching practices without connection to the oppressive conditions in which these children live'' (p. 83). In my view, making the ''connection to the oppressive conditions'' is one way of harmonizing the claims of Truth and of the Other: In this case the Other *needs* to know the Truth. My overall point, however, is the larger one that the two poles of obligation might easily diverge; thus, to use the colloquialism, a teacher may find herself having to ''fish or cut bait.'' Truth might be liberating or cruel, good politics or bad. Teachers, however, are obliged to reckon with it either way.

11. Uncharacteristic of her usually admirably clear and open style of

presentation, Noddings "argues" *ad hominem* that substantive objections to her view of this relationship between student and subject matter are "ideological" and hence nor worthy of being addressed. Period. (Noddings, 1992).

12. Perhaps the oldest surviving philosophical fragment from the pre-Socratic Greeks attests to something like this. Anaximander (b. ca. 612 B.C., fl. 560 B.C.) is said to have written that ". . . the source from which existing things derive their existence is also that to which they return at their destruction, according to necessity; for they give justice and make reparation to one another for their injustice, according to the arrangement of Time" (Quoted in Freeman, 1948, p. 19).

13. This is an account of Michel Foucault's last lecture course. Foucault distinguishes between the parrhesiast, who runs a risk in decloaking power relations, and the teacher-technician who tells truth in a safer, less divisive, mode, as just two of four truth-telling modes. "The prophet" and "the sage" are the other two (Flynn, 1988, p. 104).

14. The moral balancing act I am recommending is not unprecedented. In a more general but related context, see Susan Wolf (1990): "Seeing the world correctly, as I understand it, involves seeing not only what is true and false but also what is valuable and worthless. That is why, in describing what is required for responsibility, I have spoken of the ability to act in accordance with the True *and the Good*" (p. 118). In education, any conception of "the Good" must so clearly involve "the Other" that Wolf's point may be applied fairly directly. Even outside education, any conception of the Good not centrally concerned with others in some way—some extreme form of egoism or solipsism—is so exotic that, while it may hold an interest for specialists in philosophical ethics, it may be safely discounted here.

15. Heidegger would himself recoil at this interpretation and would no doubt see it as a form of groundless moralizing. This may just mean that Heidegger was wrong about the moral significance of his own ideas, as a long line of otherwise sympathetic commentators have held. Given Heidegger's Nazi affiliations (see Ott, 1993), the need for politicomoral critique should hardly be surprising.

16. I am using the term "personage" and calling him a "patron saint" to underscore how I wish to avoid any historical-philological debate about who Socrates actually was, whether he really said what Plato attributes to him, and so on. To me it does not much matter; I am quite content with a Socrates who is Plato's literary creation if it comes to that. I am happy, in other words, to perpetrate some mythmaking; we need our heroes, and Socrates—whoever he was or was not historically—ought to be one of them.

17. As dramatized in the *Crito*, for example, Socrates refuses to be pulled from the mood of anxiety by wishing for the escape that is offered; he thereby rejects the forgetfulness of death engendered by "the they" (das Man). In both the *Apology* and *Crito*, he attempts to soothe his friends' fretfulness over his situation by, among other things, reminding them not to heed what "everyone" thinks, what public opinion would make of it all.

CHAPTER 4

1. This is from the famous editorial—reprinted each Christmas by many newspapers for nearly a century—by Francis Pharcellus Church, originally published in the *New York Sun*, September 21, 1897.

2. For a lineup of other possible candidates, see Postman (1995) and May (1991). Though it does not mention immortality as such, Postman's book is as close to my thesis as any I have seen; it is a masterful and accessible rendering of these very themes—in a certain way, I would venture, a companion to mine.

3. The phrase "fusion of horizons" is meant to overcome the narrowly psychologistic (i.e., having to do with personal beliefs) account of earlier hermeneutics. The term *horizon* is from Husserl, where it is also meant to express the region of our intentionality in perception (in both spatial and temporal senses). For Gadamer, the term is broadened and expresses one's historical and cultural situatedness, as well as the context-bound character of interpretation. For Gadamer, our horizon "moves with us" as we gain in understanding; never is it something we can leave behind.

4. The best account of dialogue in education, one largely sympathetic to Gadamer and the play analogy, is Burbules (1993), though that author would, I think, take exception to some of my larger purposes for the notion.

5. This is an allusion to Hegel's (1821/1952) *The Philosophy of Right* and its often-misunderstood statement from the famous "Preface": "To recognize reason as the rose in the cross of the present and thereby to enjoy the present, this is the rational insight which reconciles us to the actual, the reconciliation which philosophy affords to those in whom there has once arisen an inner voice bidding them to comprehend, not only to dwell in what is substantive while still retaining subjective freedom, but also to possess subjective freedom while standing not in anything particular and accidental but in what exists absolutely" (p. 12). It would of course take more space than is possible here to explicate this quotation fully, but suffice it to say that if this indicates conservatism, it is conservatism of a most peculiar sort—altogether more peculiar than that of today's "conservatives." For a lengthy defense of Hegel along these lines, see, inter alia, Solomon (1983). The translator's footnote suggests that Hegel borrowed the rosy cross imagery from the Rosicrucians (Hegel, 1821/1952, p. 303, n. 34). In general, though, I do not mean to endorse Hegel *en bloc*—far from it. The image, though, seems to me both apt and particularly striking in the present context.

CHAPTER 5

1. Schama (1995) notes: 'The two modern careers of Mircea Eliade and Joseph Campbell are alarming cautionary tales. Campbell, the best-known mythographer in American thanks to public television, was, it now seems,

not only a student but a devotee of heroic archetypes and decidedly impatient with the quotidian littleness of democracy. Eliade, without question the most distinguished scholarly interpreter of myth, turns out to have been damningly implicated in the most brutal authoritarian politics in his native Romania" (p. 133). Schama cites as sources Lefkowitz (1990) and Manea (1991).

2. This process is argued to be more characteristic of oral cultures than literate ones, as famously argued in Havelock (1963) and Ong (1982). After exploring the example of Homer and other "oral performers" in ancient Greece, Ong continues: "The editors of *The Mwindo epic* ([Biebuyk and Mateene], 1971, p. 37) call attention to a similar strong identification of Candi Rureke, the performer of the epic, and through him of his listeners, with the hero Mwindo, an identification which actually affects the grammar of the narration, so that on occasion the narrator slips into the first person when describing the actions of the hero. So bound together are narrator, audience, and character that Rureke has the epic character Mwindo himself address the scribes taking down Rureke's performance: 'Scribe, march!' or 'O scribe you, you see that I am already going.' In the sensibility of the narrator and his audience the hero of the oral performance assimilates into the oral world even the transcribers who are de-oralizing it into text" (p. 46).

3. In a related context, see also Killilea (1988).

References

Adams, H. (1990). *The education of Henry Adams*. New York: Vintage Books. (Original work published 1907)

Adler, M. (1982). *The paideia proposal: An educational manifesto*. New York: Macmillan.

Arcilla, R. (1995). *For the love of perfection: Richard Rorty and liberal education*. New York: Routledge.

Arendt, H. (1958). *The human condition*. Chicago: University of Chicago Press.

Ariès, P. (1981). *The hour of our death* (H. Weaver, Trans.). Oxford: Oxford University Press.

Aristotle. (1984). *The complete works of Aristotle* (Vols. I and II) (J. Barnes, Ed.). Princeton: Princeton University Press.

Ayers, W. (1993). *To teach: The journey of a teacher*. New York: Teachers College Press.

Baier, A. (1995). The need for more than justice. In V. Held (Ed.), *Justice and care: Essential readings in feminist ethics* (pp. 47–58). Boulder, CO: Westview.

Barnes, J. (1988). Hellenistic philosophy and science. In J. Boardman et al. (Eds.), *Greece and the Hellenistic world* (pp. 360–375). New York: Oxford University Press.

Bauman, Z. (1992). *Mortality, immortality and other life strategies*. Stanford, CA: Stanford University Press.

Bernal, M. (1987). *Black Athena: The Afroasiatic roots of classical civilization*. New Brunswick, NJ: Rutgers University Press.

Bernstein, R. (1994). *Dictatorship of virtue: Multiculturalism and the battle for America's future*. New York: Knopf.

Biebuyk, D., & Mateene, K. (Eds. & Trans.). (1971). *The Mwindo epic from the Banyanga*. Berkeley: University of California Press.

Bissoondial, C. (1993). *Revisions to previous journal entries*. Unpublished manuscript, class assignment for EAF 421 (Blacker), Illinois State University, December 1993.

Blackburn, G. (1985). *Education in the Third Reich: A study of race and history in Nazi textbooks*. Albany: State University of New York Press.

Blacker, D. (1996). Teaching in troubled times: Democratic education and the problem of "extra people." *Teacher educator, 23*(1), 62–72.

Bluebond-Langer, M. (1980). *The private worlds of dying children*. Princeton, NJ: Princeton University Press.

Blum, L. (1994). *Moral perception and particularity*. New York: Cambridge University Press.

Borges, J. (1995). All our yesterdays (R. Mezey, Trans.). *New York Review of Books, XLII*(20), 16. (Original work published 1975)

Boyer, P. (1985). *By the bomb's early light: American thought and culture at the dawn of the atomic age.* New York: Pantheon.

Buber, M. (1958). *I and Thou* (R. Smith, Trans.). New York: Charles Scribner Sons. (Original work published 1923).

Burbules, N. (1993). *Dialogue in teaching: Theory and practice.* New York: Teachers College Press.

Burns, R. (1969). *Poems and songs* (T. Kinsley, Ed.). New York: Oxford University Press. (Original work published 1785)

Bury, J. B. (1975). *History of Greece* (rev. ed.). London: Macmillan.

Caes, C. (1985). *Beyond time: Ideas of the great philosophers on eternal existence and immortality.* Lanham, MD: University Press of America.

Callan, E. (1992). Finding a common voice. *Educational Theory, 42*(4), 429–441.

Campbell, J. (1949). *The hero with a thousand faces.* Princeton, NJ: Princeton University Press.

Campbell, J. (1988). *The power of myth* (B. Flowers, Ed.). New York: Doubleday.

Colby, A., & Kohlberg, L. (1987). *The measurement of moral judgment.* Cambridge, UK: Cambridge University Press.

Cremin, L. (1988). *American education: The metropolitan experience 1876–1980.* New York: Harper & Row.

Cuban, L. (1993). *How teachers taught: Constancy and change in America's classrooms, 1880–1990* (2nd ed.). New York: Teachers College Press.

Davidson, D. (1984). *Inquiries into truth and interpretation.* Oxford: Clarendon Press.

Derrida, J. (1995). *The gift of death* (D. Wills, Trans.). Chicago: University of Chicago Press.

Dewey, J. (1916). *Democracy and education.* New York: The Free Press.

Dicter, S. (1989). *Teachers: Straight talk from the trenches.* Los Angeles: Lowell House.

Diels, H., & Kranz, W. (1952). *Die Fragmente der Borsokratiker* [Fragments of the pre-Socratics] (Vol. II). Berlin: Weidmann.

Dijksterjuis, E. (1961). *The mechanization of the world picture* (C. Dikshoorn, Trans.). New York: Oxford University Press.

Elgort, A. (Producer & Director). (1993). *Texas tenor: The Illinois Jacquet story.* [Film]. (Available from The Jazz Store, P. O. Box 917-I, Upper Montclair, NJ 07043-0917)

Eliade, M. (1954). *The myth of the eternal return or, cosmos and history* (W. Trask, Trans.). Princeton, NJ: Princeton University Press.

Eliade, M. (1958). *Rites and symbols of initiation: The mysteries of birth and rebirth.* New York: Harper and Row.

Eliade, M. (1960). *Myths, dreams and mysteries* (P. Mairet, Trans.). New York: Harper & Row.

Eliade, M. (1965). *The two and the one* (J. Cohen, Trans.). New York: Harper & Row.

Elias, N. (1985). *The loneliness of the dying* (E. Jephcott, Trans.). Oxford: Blackwell.

Enzensberger, H. (1993). *Civil wars: From L. A. to Bosnia.* New York: The Free Press.

Flynn, T. (1988). Foucault as parrhesiast: His last lecture course at the College de France. In J. Bernauer & D. Rasumussen (Eds.), *The final Foucault* (pp. 102–118). Cambridge, MA: MIT Press.

Ford, R. (1986). *The sportswriter.* New York: Vintage.

Freeman, K. (1948). *Ancilla to the pre-Socratic philosophers.* Cambridge, MA: Harvard University Press.

Freire, P. (1970). *Pedagogy of the oppressed* (M. Ramos, Trans.). New York: Continuum.

Gadamer, H.-G. (1976). Man and language. In D. E. Linge (Trans. and Ed.), *Philosophical hermeneutics* (pp. 59–68). Berkeley: University of California Press.

Gadamer, H.-G. (1980). The proofs of immortality in Plato's *Phaedo.* In P. Smith (Ed.), *Dialogue and dialectic: Eight hermeneutical studies on Plato* (pp. 21–38). New Haven, CT: Yale University Press.

Gadamer, H.-G. (1989a). Text and interpretation. In D. Michelfelder & R. Palmer (Eds.), *Dialogue and deconstruction: The Gadamer-Derrida encounter.* Albany, NY: State University of New York Press.

Gadamer, H.-G. (1989b). *Truth and method.* J. Weinsheimer & D. Marshall (Trans. & Rev.). New York: Crossroads.

Gallagher, S. (1992). *Hermeneutics and education.* Albany: State University of New York Press.

Galston, W. (1989). Civic education in the liberal state. In N. Rosenblum (Ed.), *Liberalism and the moral life* (pp. 89–101). Cambridge, MA: Harvard University Press.

Gardner, H. (1983). *Frames of mind: The theory of multiple intelligences.* New York: Basic Books.

Gardner, H. (1993). *Multiple intelligences: The theory in practice.* New York: Basic Books.

Garland, R. (1985). *The Greek way of death.* Ithaca, NY: Cornell University Press.

Gilligan, C. (1982). *In a different voice: Psychological theory and women's development.* Cambridge, MA: Harvard University Press.

Gitlin, A., & Margonis, F. (1995). The political aspect of reform: Teacher resistance as good sense. *American Journal of Education, 103*(4), 377–390.

Gitlin, T. (1995). *Twilight of common dreams: Why America is wracked by culture wars.* New York: Metropolitan Books.

Haar, M. (1993). *Heidegger and the essence of man* (W. McNeill, Trans.). Albany, NY: State University of New York Press.

Haines, R. (Director). (1991). *The doctor.* Burbank, CA: Touchstone Pictures.

Havelock, E. (1963). *Preface to Plato.* Cambridge, MA: Harvard University Press.

Heidegger, M. (1959). *Introduction to metaphysics.* New Haven, CT: Yale University Press.

Heidegger, M. (1962a). *Being and time* (J. Macquarrie & E. Robinson, Trans.). New York: Harper & Row.

Heidegger, M. (1962b). *Kant and the problem of metaphysics* (J. Churchill, Trans.). Bloomington, IN: Indiana University Press.

Heidegger, M. (1968). *What is called thinking?* (J. Gray, Trans.). New York: Harper & Row.

Heidegger, M. (1977a). Letter on humanism (F. Capuzzi & J. Gray, Trans.). In D. Krell (Ed.), *Martin Heidegger: Basic writings* (pp. 193–242). New York: Harper & Row.

Heidegger, M. (1977b). The question concerning technology. In W. Lovitt (Trans. & Ed.), *The question concerning technology and other essays* (pp. 3–35). New York: Harper Torchbooks.

Hegel, G. W. F. (1952). *The philosophy of right* (T. Knox, Trans.). New York: Oxford University Press. (Original work published 1821).

Hegel, G. W. F. (1977). *Phenomenology of spirit* (A. Miller, Trans.). New York: Oxford University Press. (Original work published 1807)

Herf, J. (1984). *Reactionary modernism: Technology, culture and politics in Weimar and the Third Reich.* New York: Cambridge University Press.

Hirsch, E. D., Jr. (1987). *Cultural literacy: What every American needs to know.* New York: Houghton Mifflin.

Hoffman, B. (1972). *Albert Einstein, creator and rebel.* New York: Plume.

Hölderlin, F. (1990). The Rhine. In (D. Constantine, Trans.), *Selected poems* (pp. 33–38). Newcastle Upon Tyne: Bloodaxe Books.

Homer. (1993). *The Odyssey* (A. Cook, Trans. & Ed.). New York: Norton.

Horkheimer, M. (1974). *Eclipse of reason.* New York: Continuum.

Horkheimer, M., & Adorno, T. (1972). *Dialectic of enlightenment.* New York: Continuum.

Houston, J. (1996). *A mythic life: Learning to live our greater story.* San Francisco: HarperSanFrancisco.

Husserl, E. (1976). *Ideas: A general introduction to pure phenomenology* (W. Boyce, Trans.). New York: Humanities Press.

Ingram, D. (1984). Hermeneutics and truth. *Journal of the British Society for Phenomenology, 15*(1), 65–85.

Irigaray, L. (1994). Sorcerer's love: A reading of Plato's *Symposium*, Diotima's speech (E. H. Kuykendall, Trans.). In N. Tuana (Ed.), *Feminist interpretations of Plato* (pp. 180–200). University Park, PA: Pennsylvania State University Press.

Irwin, T. H. (1977). *Plato's moral thoery: The early and middle dialogues.* Oxford: Oxford University Press.

Irwin, T. H. (1989). *Classical thought.* New York: Oxford University Press.

Jackson, P. W. (1992). *Untaught lessons.* New York: Teachers College Press.

Jaeger, W. (1944). *Paideia: The ideals of Greek culture* (Vol. III). (G. Highet, Trans.). New York: Oxford University Press.

Joyce, J. (1986). *Ulysses* (H. Gabler, Ed.). New York: Random House. (Original work published 1922)

Jung, C. J. (1959). *The archetypes and the collective unconscious* (R. Hull, Trans.). Princeton, NJ: Princeton University Press.

Jünger, E. (1922). *Der Kampf als inneres Erlebnis* [War as the deepest experience]. Berlin: E. S. Mittler & Sohn.

Jünger, E. (1972). Technology as the mobilization of the world through the *Gestalt* of the worker (J. Vincent, Trans.), with R. Rundell (Rev.). In C. Mitcham & R. Mackey (Eds.), *Philosophy and technology: Readings in the philosophical problems of technology* (pp. 269–289). New York: The Free Press. (Original work published 1932)

Kanpol, B., & Yeo, F. (1995). Inner-city realities: Democracy within difference, theory and practice. *The Urban Review, 27*(1), 77–91.

Kerferd, G. B. (1981). *The sophistic movement*. New York: Cambridge University Press.

Killilea, A. (1988). *The politics of being mortal*. Lexington: University of Kentucky Press.

Kohlberg, L. (1987). *Child psychology and childhood education*. New York: Longman.

Koskinski, J. (1970). *Being there*. New York: Harcourt Brace Jovanovich.

Kundera, M. (1992). *Immortality*. New York: HarperColllins.

Kymlicka, W. (1990). *Contemporary political philosophy: An introduction*. New York: Oxford University Press.

Lefkowitz, M. (1990). The myth of Joseph Campbell. *American Scholar, 59*(3), 429–434.

Lefkowitz, M. (1996). *Not out of Africa: How Afrocentrism became an excuse to teach myth as history*. New York: Basic Books.

Lesy, M. (1989). *The forbidden zone*. New York: Anchor.

Levertov, D. (1995). The beginning of wisdom. *American Poetry Review, 24* (5), 3.

Levinas, E. (1989). Ethics as first philosophy (S. Hand, Trans.). In S. Hand (Ed.), *The Levinas reader* (pp. 75–87). Oxford: Blackwell.

Levine, M. (1992). The use and abuse of *Black Athena. American Historical Review, 97*(2), 440–460.

Lifton, R. (1987). *The future of immortality and other essays for the nuclear age*. New York: Basic Books.

Lind, M. (1995). *The next American nation: The new nationalism and the fourth American revolution*. New York: The Free Press.

Lucretius. (1951). *On the nature of the universe* (R. Latham, Trans.). New York: Penguin.

Malcolm X, as told to A. Haley. (1965). *The autobiography of Malcolm X*. New York: Grove.

Manea, N. (1991, August 5). Happy guilt. The New Republic, 27–36.

Marrou, H. I. (1956). *A history of education in antiquity* (G. Lamb, Trans.). Madison: University of Wisconsin Press.

Matthews, G. (1994). *Philosophy of childhood*. Cambridge, MA: Harvard University Press.

May, R. (1991). *The cry for myth*. New York: Norton.

McPherran, M. (1994). Socrates on the immortality of the soul. *Journal of the History of Philosophy, 32*(1), 1–22.

Melling, D. (1987). *Understanding Plato.* Oxford: Oxford University Press.

Mighton, J. (1995). Artistic immortality. *Common Knowledge, 4*(2), 108–112.

Mogilka, J. (1994, November). *Four ways of dying: Art lessons for the foundations.* Paper presented at the annual meeting of the American Educational Studies Association, Chapel Hill, NC.

Moore, C. (1963). *Ancient beliefs in the immortality of the soul.* New York: Cooper Square Publishers.

Nagel, T. (1979). *Mortal questions.* New York: Cambridge University Press.

Nietzsche, F. (1954). *Thus spoke Zarathustra* (W. Kaufmann, Trans.). New York: Penguin. (Original work published 1892)

Neitzsche, F. (1974). *The gay science* (W. Kaufmann, Trans.). New York: Vintage Books. (Original work published 1887)

Nietzsche, F. (1982). The wanderer and his shadow. In W. Kaufmann (Ed.), *The portable Nietzsche* (pp. 70–71). New York: Penguin Books. (Original work published 1880)

Noddings, N. (1984). *Caring: A feminine approach to ethics and moral education.* Berkeley: University of California Press.

Noddings, N. (1992). *The challenge to care in schools.* New York: Teachers College Press.

Nuland, S. (1994). *How we die: Reflections on life's final chapter.* New York: Vintage.

Nussbaum, M. (1994). *The therapy of desire: Theory and practice in Hellenistic ethics.* Princeton, NJ: Princeton University Press.

Oakeshott, M. (1989). Education: The engagement and its frustration. In T. Fuller (Ed.), *The voice of liberal learning: Michael Oakeshott on education* (pp. 63–94). New Haven, CT: Yale University Press.

O'Connor, D. (1994). The erotic self-sufficiency of Socrates: A reading of Xenophon's *Memorabilia.* In P. A. Vander Waerdt (Ed.), *The Socratic movement* (pp. 151–180). Ithaca, NY: Cornell University Press.

O'Connor, D. (1996). Longing for the present: Or, teaching without a future. In A. Neiman (Ed.), *Philosophy of Education 1995* (pp. 208–209). Urbana, IL: Philosophy of Education Society.

Okin, S. (1989a). *Justice, gender, and the family.* New York: Basic Books.

Okin, S. (1989b). Reason and feeling in thinking about justice. *Ethics, 99*(2), 219–249.

Olan, L. (1971). *Judaism and immortality.* New York: Union of American Hebrew Congregations.

Ong, W. (1982). *Orality and literacy: The technologizing of the word.* New York: Routledge.

Ott, H. (1993). *Martin Heidegger: A political life* (A. Blunden, Trans.). New York: Basic Books.

Pagels, H. (1982). *The cosmic code: Quantum physics as the language of nature.* New York: Simon & Schuster.

Patterson, R. (1965). *Plato on immortality.* University Park: Pennsylvania State University Press.

Paulos, J. (1989). *Innumeracy: Mathematical illiteracy and its consequences.* New York: Hill & Wang.

Paxton, F. (1990). *Christianizing death: The creation of a ritual process in early medieval Europe*. Ithaca, NY: Cornell Univesity Press.

Peters, R. S. (1973). The justification of education. In R. S. Peters (Ed.), *The philosophy of education* (pp. 239–267). New York: Oxford University Press.

Plato. (1956). *Protagoras and Meno* (W. K. C. Guthrie, Trans.). New York: Penguin.

Plato. (1974). *Plato's Republic* (G.M.A. Grube, Trans.). Indianapolis: Hackett.

Plato. (1981). *Five dialogues*: Euthyphro, Apology, Crito, Meno, Phaedo (G. M. A. Grube, Trans.). Indianapolis: Hackett.

Plato. (1989). *The collected dialogues of Plato, including the Letters* (E. Hamilton & H. Cairns, Eds.). Princeton, NJ: Princeton University Press.

Postman, Neil. (1995). *The end of education: Redefining the value of school*. New York: Knopf.

Reich, R. (1991). *The work of nations: Preparing ourselves for 21st century capitalism*. New York: Knopf.

Robinson, T. E., & Brower, W. A. (1982). Teachers and their survivors. *Phi Delta Kappan, 63*(10), 714–720.

Rodd, I. (1992). McLunchrooms! *The Nation, 255*(8), 276.

Roethke, T. (1975). *The collected poems of Theodore Roethke*. New York: Anchor Books/Doubleday.

Rorty, R. (1995). Untruth and consequences. *The New Republic, 213*(5), 213–215.

Sartre, J. P. (1964). *Nausea* (L. Alexander, Trans.). New York: New Directions. (Original work published 1938)

Schama, S. (1995). *Landscape and memory*. New York: Knopf.

Scheffler, I. (1960). *The language of education*. Springfield, IL: Thomas.

Schleiermacher, F. (1977). Uber den Begriff der hermeneutic mit Bezug auf F. A. Wolfs Andeutungen und Asts Lehrbuch [On the concept of hermeneutics in the work of F. A. Wolf and Asts]. In M. Frank (Ed.), *Hermeneutic und Kritik* [Hermeneutics and Culture]. Frankfurt: Suhrkamp. (Original work published 1835)

Schlesinger, Jr., A. (1992). *The disuniting of America: Reflections on a multicultural society*. New York: Norton.

Seebohm, T. (1992). Falsehood as the prime mover of hermeneutics. *Journal of Speculative Philosophy, 6*, 1–24.

Silin, J. (1995). *Sex, death, and the education of children: Our passion for ignorance in the age of AIDS*. New York: Teachers College Press.

Solomon, R. (1983). *In the spirit of Hegel: A study of G.W.F.'s Phenomenology of Spirit*. New York: Oxford University Press.

Soltis, J. (1968). *An introduction to the analysis of educational concepts*. Reading, MA: Addison-Wesley.

Stern, K. (1996). *A force upon the plain: The American militia movement and the politics of hate*. New York: Simon & Schuster.

Stern, P. (1993). *Socratic rationalism and political philosophy: An interpretation of Plato's Phaedo*. Albany: State University of New York Press.

Striker, G. (1990). *Ataraxia*: Happiness as tranquillity. *Monist 73*(1), 97–110.

Tóth, E. (1995). Van Gogh gives evidence (P. Jay, Trans.). *American Poetry Review, 24*(1), 36.

Tronto, J. (1993). *Moral boundaries: A political argument for an ethic of care.* New York: Routledge.

Tronto, J. (1995). Women and caring: What can feminists learn about morality from caring? In (V. Held, Ed.), *Justice and care: Essential readings in feminist ethics* (pp. 101–116). Boulder, CO: Westview Press.

Vermeule, E. (1979). *Aspects of death in early Greek art and poetry.* Berkeley: University of California Press.

Vlastos, G. (1981). *Platonic studies* (2nd ed.). Princeton, NJ: Princeton University Press.

Vlastos, G. (1990). *Socrates, ironist and moral philosopher.* Ithaca, NY: Cornell University Press.

Warnke, G. (1987). *Gadamer: Hermeneutics, tradition, reason.* Stanford: Stanford University Press.

Warnock, M. (1992). *The uses of philosophy.* Oxford: Blackwell.

Weinberg, S. (1993). *Dreams of a final theory: The scientist's search for the ultimate laws of nature.* New York: Vintage.

White, E. B. (1952). *Charlotte's web.* New York: Harper & Row.

Williams, B. (1972). *Morality: An introduction to ethics.* Cambridge, UK: Cambridge University Press.

Wolf, S. (1990). *Freedom within reason.* New York: Oxford University Press.

Yee, S. (1990). *Careers in the classroom: When teaching is more than a job.* New York: Teachers College Press.

Zimmerman, M. (1990). *Heidegger's confrontation with modernity: Technology, politics, art.* Bloomington: Indiana Unversity Press.

Index

About the Author

David Blacker is Assistant Professor in the Department of Educational Administration and Foundations at Illinois State University. He received his PhD in the philosophy of education from the University of Illinois at Urbana-Champaign in 1994. His work has appeared in *The Journal of Speculative Philosophy, Educational Theory, Philosophy of Education, Educational Foundations, The Teacher Educator, Religious Education, The American Journal of Education,* and other publications.